SPARK

Be More Innovative Through Co-Creation

JOHN WINSOR

Dearborn™
Trade Publishing

A **Kaplan Professional** Company

President, Dearborn Publishing: Roy Lipner
Vice President and Publisher: Cynthia A. Zigmund
Senior Acquisitions Editor: Michael Cunningham
Designer: Steve Jenkins

Published by Dearborn Trade Publishing
A Kaplan Professional Company

Printed in the United States of America

06 07 08 10 9 8 7 6 5 4 3 2 1

Library of Congress Cataloging-in-Publication Data

Winsor, John, 1959-
    Spark : be more innovative through co-creation / John Winsor.
      p. cm.
    Includes index.
    ISBN 1-4195-0316-2 (5x7.375 hardcover)
  1. Relationship marketing. 2. Customer relations. 3. Product management. I. Title.
    HF5415.55.W56 2005
    658.8'12—dc22

2005015087

To the Garage – Where great ideas are sparked.
(This is my garage and the home of a couple of start-up companies.)

How to Use Spark

Welcome to *Spark*. Come on in! This book is about innovation – meaningful innovation that comes from co-creating with your customers and your fellow employees. *Spark* was written to inspire you to think about innovation in new ways. To do that, I have gathered several perspectives on the subject, and, appropriately, this book also uses an innovative structure and design.

Spark is structured in four sections: Section One – "The Team"; Section Two – "The Company"; Section Three – "The Customer"; and Section Four – "The Culture." Each of these sections represents a different piece of the innovation ecosystem. Successful innovation happens in the zone where these four pieces of the ecosystem intersect and overlap.

Within each section there are four chapters; the chapters, in turn, have four segments, including "Inspiration," "Tools," "Interaction," and "Resources." The Inspiration segment is a personal interview that offers one perspective on a unique innovation issue. The Tools segment in each chapter presents ideas on how to put some of the ideas discussed into action. Interaction prompts readers to join in the co-creative process – each Interaction segment poses a provocative question or exercise and space to draw or write down your thoughts. There is also an online component to this section, giving readers the opportunity to form a community around the ideas

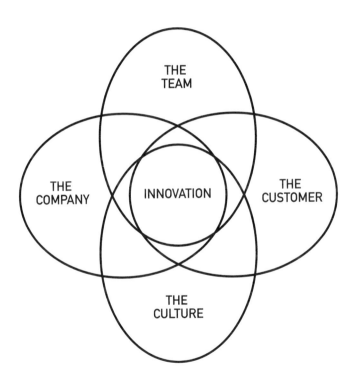

presented in *Spark* and to actively co-create new innovation solutions. Last, the Resources segment in each chapter can act as a road map for further exploration of the subjects discussed.

Along this journey of innovation, I consciously set some rules for myself:

Innovation at Every Level — *Spark* was not written just for CEOs or innovation teams. I did not set out to have conversations with "rock star" innovators. Every person within an organization can find interesting ways to be innovative.

Not Just Technology — I consciously left out technology companies for the simple reason that throughout our conversations, the point was often made that many technology companies *exist* for the sake of innovation, regardless of their profitability. Most companies don't have the option to be unprofitable. I focused on the *process* of being innovative, which can be applied across any industry, from manufacturing to technology.

Inspiration Is Everywhere — The people I chose to participate in this book are all people I know well who have inspired me in various ways. Being innovative is not a holy grail – it is all around us. Instead of being separated from innovative thinkers by six degrees, innovative thought and becoming more innovative yourself might lie only one degree away. I want to encourage readers to learn from others who are nearby and accessible.

Spark's primary goal is to be a resource. I hope it can become an innovation journal for you, and you will be inspired by the wonderful people who have participated in it. So, make Spark yours. Write in it. Draw in it. Tape stuff to it. Rip it up! But most of all, have fun with it! Become an active part of the Spark community. Enjoy.

The Story Behind *Spark*

I was recently in Kenya with my family when I had an experience that made me rethink the mechanics of innovation. We were on safari in a game reserve called Lewa Downs. One evening, we watched three cheetahs hunting. Cheetahs are beautiful, sleek animals; at 75 to 120 pounds, they are small by African cat standards. They are quite ferocious, typically solitary animals that are able to run 70 miles an hour to catch their prey. When hunting, they are dependent on these great bursts of speed. Yet the energy needed to run this fast can sometimes overwhelm them, requiring several hours of rest to regain enough energy to hunt again. This energy expenditure, coupled with their timid nature among other animals, often causes cheetahs to leave a kill if a lion or hyena challenges them.

The three cheetahs we saw hunting together looked unusual compared to other cheetahs we had observed. It seems that these three young cheetahs, all brothers, had formed an alliance. Not only did they still live together at the age of 5, but they hunted together as well. This organized effort of hunting gave the brothers a great advantage. First, they could hunt while expending much less energy, using tactics that incorporated all of their skills. Second, no lion or hyena was going to mess with them when they had made a kill. Hence, they also ate more than the average cheetah by forming an alliance and being innovative. As a result, these three cheetahs looked more like leopards and weighed 50 percent more than the average cheetah. These brothers had figured out intuitively that if they shared the responsibility of hunting, they would have a better chance of surviving and thriving on the African plains. In observing them, I realized that innovation is not something that is exclusive to business but is important to every living thing as it tries to adapt to a changing environment and survive. Often by forming an alliance or community around a challenge and by co-creating a solution with others, the opportunity to be successful increases dramatically.

The drive to be more innovative has been hoisted onto the shoulders of all companies because, in fact, everyone is affected by broader innovations such as the Internet and information technology. This has created a hypercompetitive marketplace, where the linear work processes of the industrial age are being replaced by the nonlinear paradigm of the information age. Hence, just like the cheetahs, being innovative is not an option; it is imperative to survive in our radically changing world.

As humans, we are all innovative by nature. We have the innate ability to adapt to our ever-changing environment. Unfortunately, much like intuition, our ability to innovate has diminished as we have learned to adapt to the more linear needs of our modern culture. Likewise at work, our ability to be innovative has been slowly stripped away, replaced instead by mechanics of the modern work environment and the need to get things done in a timely and predictable fashion.

To be innovative, we must capture the sense of wonder and possibility we all had as children. We must unlearn many of the more linear processes that inhibit our ability and flexibility to be more creative and innovative.

But in the context of work, what does innovation really mean? I've always liked Peter Drucker's take on innovation: "Innovation is the specific instrument of entrepreneurship. The act that endows resources with a new capacity to create wealth." Today, companies must strive to be more entrepreneurial, moving faster to survive and thrive.

To understand the tremendous pressure our changing world has put on companies and people in their efforts to sustain that entrepreneurial spirit, our Radar team interviewed a number of people we feel are truly innovative. We discovered in the interviews that there is a difference between generating innovation, creating an innovative product or service, and being innovative.

Typically, the people we all think of as innovative are following their own path creatively, being entrepreneurs, engineers, or artists, going against the grain not only of the markets they work in but also of what might be seen as "best practices." They work everywhere, from big companies to small studios. The common traits these people share are a willingness to accept that they live in a rapidly changing environment and the necessity of engaging with others to thrive in today's chaos. Co-creation manifests itself differently for everyone. For some, it is a deep engagement with their internal team; for others, it is engaging with customers and the culture in which they live.

Co-creation is the whole point of *Spark*. In fact, *Spark* is not only *about* co-creation, but it was in fact co-created by many innovative voices. One thing that drove me to write this book was to better understand the *magic* that infuses innovation. I wanted to talk to people who not only innovate but also lead innovative lives. I've always felt that the fundamental idea of co-creation – that it takes more than one brilliant mind to make an innovation happen – is an essential element in business.

Even after starting ten magazines and four companies and writing a few books, I remain entranced by the magic and the power of co-creation. Each time, there was a spark in the darkness, a connection. It *always* started with that connection to somebody else.

The Team

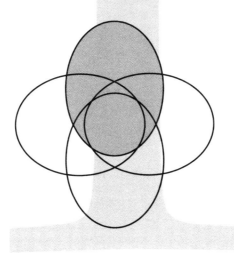

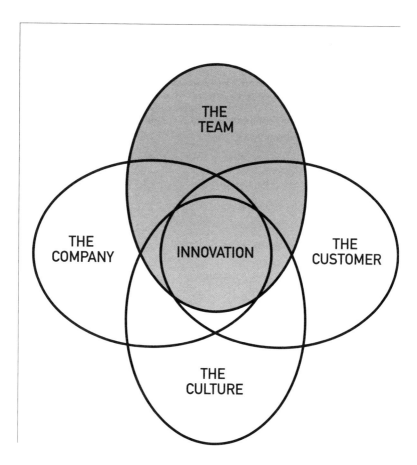

The basis of co-creating innovation with your team is the concept of dialogue. To become more skilled in fully participating in a dialogue, you and your team members must discover what currently limits your learning. You must be able to uncover your own assumptions and beliefs that contribute to the behaviors of everyone else on the team. Once these behaviors are understood, they must be evolved.

The four chapters in this section, "Be More Human," "Communicate Faster," "Follow Your Intuition," and "Break Out of Your Routine," should inspire you to find new ways to create a deeper and more thoughtful dialogue around the challenges of innovation. The interviews with Johnnie Moore, Rob DeFlorio, Matt Jacobson, and Jeff Garwood will encourage you to think about the way that you and your team interact and give you new tools to be innovative.

The goal, through dialogue, is to develop a new level of trust that can promote deeper cooperation, allowing you to be more productive in your search for innovation. The real outcome of greater cooperation is developing a fine-tuned intuition about the problems and opportunities surrounding innovation for your company and team.

4

I first met Johnnie, a branding consultant based in London, on a videoconference call to discuss our participation in the BrandShift weblog. I was a little nervous going into the meeting, knowing that I was by far the most junior in a group of experienced bloggers that included Jennifer Rice, Andrew Lark, Alex Williams, and Hylton Joliffe. For a long while during the call I simply listened, feeling very intimidated by the team's obvious knowledge of basic blogging ideas and terms that I did not understand at all. It wasn't until Johnnie introduced some of the principles of "improv" that I felt comfortable engaging in the conversation. This idea of allowing everybody to participate in a positive dialogue, regardless of the level of knowledge, really intrigued me.

Following my interview with Johnnie, the magic of improv really started to become apparent to me. I had posted a provocative thought on my own weblog and received a couple of sarcastic and aggressive responses. Being a person who always wants to be liked and doesn't deal with conflict very well, I was unsure how to respond. I have always had difficulty understanding how to deal with aggressively differing opinions. And often these positions become calcified, creating great rifts in companies and on teams.

After Johnnie's interview and especially his idea of "Yes, and?" I was able to forge a new connection to the people on my blog who expressed radically different opinions. By saying, "I understand where you're coming from and, in fact, here's something to add," I was able to build from the areas of common understanding in a positive way, instead of focusing only on the differences. This kind of optimism can bring a lot of power to our interactions with both coworkers and customers.

I started to pay attention to improv about three or four years ago, after a friend of a friend invited me to an improv conference. I went very much on an impulse, which seems quite appropriate, really, and I immediately knew that this was a very powerful and accessible tool. It resonated with me, and I've increasingly used improv ideas and exercises in my work. Improv starts from a fundamentally optimistic assumption that people are actually good at innovating and then follows a few simple precepts to make it quite easy to create great ideas.

The Power of Relationships

The practice of improv emphasizes and recognizes the value of relationship in creating ideas. There's a stereotype of the innovative or creative person as the lonely artist, starving and alone in a garret somewhere. But what improv emphasizes is how ideas are created between people. It's not the idea of one person being added to another the way you might build a wall out of separate bricks. Improv helps us create things between us that are more than just the sum of our separate ideas. It encourages us to play together

6

and see what comes up, in a spirit of being pretty forgiving of what we might laughingly call "mistakes." We simply look to build on what's good in the creation of ideas; we throw mud at the wall – as we say in England – and see what sticks, and build on that.

Focus on the Creative Tension

A popular image of creativity is the "creative spark." Think about the ceiling of the Sistine Chapel and Michelangelo's celebrated picture of God giving life to Adam. Their fingers almost touch, and many imagine an electric spark between the finger of God and man. A spark wouldn't happen if there weren't a difference between one end of the spark and the other. It's in that gap that the potential exists. So you might call that creative tension – but the creativity happens in the gap between one charged position and another. It's much the same with improv, where the actors really commit to their positions in the improvisation and thus create that space in between. Then the spark has to cross; something has to happen in that gap that's creative. In that image, I think it's possible that both God and Man are a bit surprised by the spark. A willingness to be surprised by ourselves and others is somewhere near the heart of any creative process.

Improv helps us create things between us that are more than just the sum of our separate ideas.

Allow Creative Space

A classic improv exercise is called one-word story. One person says a word, and the other person says another word, one at a time. We have no idea where the story's going to go. But usually when people play this, they start to create some quite interesting material, make coherent sentences, and build the stories. There's goodwill between everyone and a willingness to take what's offered by another player and add to it. In that relationship, you create a story that no one player thought but that each player clearly influenced.

Improv suggests that creativity is fundamentally something that arises between people and is never done by someone on their own. Isaac Newton famously said that he stood on the shoulders of giants, acknowledging that his great thinking was only possible because of the thoughts and work of those who came before him. If our stereotype of the creative person is that solitary artist in the garret and if intellectual property is something people are very anxious to protect, it's really important to remember that creativity can't really be done by any one person on their own. People can only act in response to the stimulus that they're given.

Keep It Simple

Improv has a kind of magic to it. It just works. Improv exercises are superficially very simple. Something like the one-word story exercise is simple to the point of being pretty silly, yet most people become very engaged, very quickly. They can't help themselves from getting drawn in and trying to make it work. And they put a lot of energy into the game of making up a story together, often surprising themselves by how committed they become to wanting it to work. There's a story about Michelangelo's statue of David. Someone says, "It's quite an incredible statue – the beauty, the lines – everything about it is wonderful. How were you able to produce that?" And Michelangelo responds, "Oh, it's easy, really; I just take the stone and I chip

> It's really important to remember that creativity can't really be done by any one person on their own.

away anything that isn't David." I have that view – I think that people innately have the ability to play and create together. And it doesn't take much to bring that out in people if you strip it down to something simple. I think what improv does, by setting up these rather foolish, slightly silly games, is to immediately tap into people's innate ability to play together. You bypass all the strange behaviors that you've learned over the years regarding how to do things in teams. It helps us chip away the bits of the stone that aren't David. Something just jumps out from people when you get an improv rap going.

Improv Is Subversive

You could say that improv is quite subversive. For many people, it's just a pleasant activity – they play it and they laugh. But some people soon realize that it's actually quite challenging, quite interesting as well. Improv will start to smoke out all the rules we make up in our heads about how to behave. It makes us look at ourselves. So it works on one level by just being fun, energizing people, and breaking the ice, so people are just more playful at the end. But there's a second level, where people start to reflect on what happens in those games. I'll watch people play one-word story, and then I'll ask what they learned. They'll tell me it was fun, that perhaps they felt a bit frustrated when something didn't work so well. Then I'll ask them to think about what makes it easier to play the game and what makes it harder. What tends to emerge is the temptation for people to try to control the story; they say a word hoping the story will go in a particular direction, and then the other player says

> Improv will start to smoke out all the rules we make up in our heads about how to behave.

something unexpected. Now they're stuck because they've got this plan for the story that they now have to let go of. So I suggest to them that maybe they need to let go of planning it out in the first place and simply focus on adding the word that immediately comes to mind.

Let Go of the Goal

I think that improv, as well as being very light and fun, can be very exposing because it shows us some of the limiting ways in which we behave. If you bring all that baggage to a simple story, what kind of baggage do you bring to an issue that is really important to you? It shows how attached we can become to having our way in meetings, for instance, instead of letting go and seeing where the meeting might go.

I think there is a predisposition in Western cultures to think that we only do activities when we know what the goal is, that we won't do anything unless we know what the point is. But actually I think we all do a lot of things in a more chaotic way. We all have that childlike part that just wants to explore. We don't know what the point is other than to just see what happens. I don't know how else innovation can happen other than just trying stuff out.

> I don't know how else innovation can happen other than just trying stuff out.

Improv in Action

I've done some work with a successful boutique hotel chain that basically got some market research feedback suggesting that even though it was considered quite a cool brand, its customer service was pretty variable. It wasn't matching "soft skills" with what it was offering in terms of the coolness of the brand.

The management decided to use improv as a way to change that. They actually looked at all the other hotels that had systems for managing customer service – procedures and manuals aplenty – and these didn't really gel with this company. They thought, "Well, if we do what the others do, we won't be different from them. We'll be just doing best practice, which ends up being standard practice and the same as everybody else."

They got quite excited about improv, because it offered the chance for them to create something unique, playful, and enjoyable. So we did some improv workshops with their people, and the outcome basically allowed their staff to offer good customer service in a more playful and energetic way that was much less offensive than following a script; it's more of an adventure. Each time they meet a new customer, it's like starting a new improv. It's in the spirit of, "Well, what can we create with this customer? How can we be of service to them?"

This company used improv to differentiate itself in the most brilliant way by tapping into an endless source of difference. You're allowing yourself to create something new and authentic and different with each encounter, because you've kind of thrown away the rulebook and the standard procedures.

One simple rule is "Yes, and?" – which is basically seeing what you can take from what somebody offers you and build on it.

"Yes, and?"

The rules of thumb for improv are fantastic principles for team building and customer relationships. One simple rule is "Yes, and?" – which is basically seeing what you can take from what somebody offers you and build on it. Rather than pointing out what's wrong, you go with what's good.

Another principle is to make your partners look good; if they're complaining, look at what you can say to make them feel okay about complaining – not feel excluded but know that you're with them. In another sense, there are no rules; it's all about "What can we make up between us; what can we create as we go along; what can we co-create together?"

Another main principle is about being in the moment. A lot of people who teach improv would say that everything happens in the moment, that improv becomes real genius when people just say the very first thing that comes into their heads and just go with the moment and the spontaneous response. Most of the warm-up games in improv are about getting people just to respond more quickly, be very spontaneous – just be in the moment. I guess it's a bit like the experience some authors describe of "channeling," or what Mihaly Csikszentmihalyi calls a flow state – all David, no spare stone.

> Improv becomes real genius when people just say the very first thing that comes into their heads.

Explore Issues More Deeply

Often, just introducing some improv is enough to change the energy in a room. It's also important to allow for periods without the expectation of fireworks. It's quite natural for teams to have periods of lower energy; in improv, the response to that would be to ask, "Well, what's good about this?" In a team that has lost its passion, sometimes that's worth exploring – maybe the loss of passion has a purpose. If we ask "What's this about?" maybe it's that we want a break or maybe need to let go of trying so hard. If you look at those so-called blocks, there's often good information there. If the energy's gone down in the room, maybe it's time to do something different.

I've sometimes found in meetings that you need to get behind your frustrations. If you're stuck, really ask yourself why you don't want to work at the moment and give a voice to that. Improv is about the challenge to keep reframing what's going on; maybe we need to say, "Yes, and?" to our own frustrations. One of the reasons I think conventional brainstorming doesn't work very well is the rather simplistic idea that we must have no negative ideas. I think a sophisticated application of the "Yes, and?" principle is that ultimately it isn't an injunction to tell other people something; it's a challenge to figure out, "Well, how can I 'Yes, and?' this?"

I recently received a very critical note about an event I'd been involved with. My first response was to feel a little hurt and annoyed; then I thought that even though I might not like its overall tone, there were some really good arguments there, some ideas for things that we could do differently next time. I think that's the improv response; that if you're given a difficult customer or a difficult response, the challenge is to find a way to ask, "What is there in this that I can say yes to?"

> One of the reasons I think conventional brainstorming doesn't work very well is the rather simplistic idea that we must have no negative ideas.

Be More Human

❶ Start with an Optimistic Assumption on the Outcome – By beginning with the feeling that their team will find a solution to an innovation challenge, people can stay focused on the challenge at hand without the influence of negative energy from considering possible unsuccessful outcomes.

❷ Make More Creative Mental Space – Mental space is created when you and your team realize that the magic happens between you instead from just one person. Energy can be created by focusing on what happens between people. Think about what each person can add to make a positive contribution by building on each other's ideas.

❸ Let Go of Control – Use the one-word story game to get everyone out of the mindset of owning individual ideas. Instead, start thinking about collectively influencing the outcome. How can you stand on each other's shoulders?

❹ "Yes, and?" – Instead of using the "Yes, but" perspective of pointing out what is wrong with someone's idea, try thinking about a "Yes, and?" approach. How can you add something positive to an idea, even if it is a direct attack on you? Some call this idea "radical inclusion." This inclusion does fuel the magic of engagement.

❺ Make Your Teammates Look Good – I love working with people who make me look good; don't we all? Everyone becomes more energized, willing to step out of the comfort zone to participate and even take risks.

❻ Be in the Moment – Like many other people, it's sometimes hard for me to stay in the moment. One of the best ways to do this requires full engagement. That might mean changing the venue, rearranging the furniture, holding gatherings at odd times, or anything that can get people fully engaged in a process of innovation in the moment.

❼ Be More Playful – Everyone gets so serious at work. In most cases, only good things can happen if everyone starts having a little more fun. This begs the question: Do you live to work or work to live? If you and your team can be more playful, maybe the live/work dynamic is elevated to the point where work is another fun and engaging outlet for people's energy.

Interaction

_____

_____

_____

_____

_____

_____

_____

_____

_____

_____

_____

_____

_____

_____

_____

Be More Human

Think about an unresolved issue at work that is currently under your skin. How can the principles of improv, including "Yes, and?" help you bring the issue to a positive outcome for everyone involved?

Resources

1. Johnnie Moore's Web site: www.johnniemoore.com/blog/. Johnnie's got lots of interesting links on using improv in business as well as on many other topics.

2. "Improv Engineering" by Jean Thilmany, *Mechanical Engineering*, Management Supplement, March 2005, 7. This is an interesting look at the relationship between engineers and improvisational comedy.

3. Improv Across America: www.improvamerica.com. This site contains information about America's improv troupes, sorted by states, and includes shows, performers, festivals, and workshops.

4. Applied Improvisational Network: www.appliedimprov.net/blog/archives/2005/04/academic_resear_1.php#more. A bibliography of academic research on improv and its applications to business.

5. "60 Seconds with Second City" by Andrew Moesel, *Fast Company*, November 2003, 42. A short interview with Second City Communications President Tom Yorton, writer-actors Ed Furman and Greg Mills, and writer-director Tracy Thorpe about improv skills and humor in the workplace.

6. "Send in the Clowns" by Leigh Buchanan, *Inc.*, September 2000, 89. Another good article about Second City.

7. "Improv at the Interview" by Jennifer Merritt, *BusinessWeek*, February 3, 2003, 63. Merritt looks at how companies in the U.S. are turning to the situational interview.

8. "Improv in the Workplace," *Harvard Management Communication Letter* 4, no. 2 (February 2001): 8. Looks at the relevance of the babble games and the foursquare matrix improvisation games in establishing profound collaboration.

9. *Tales for Change: Using Storytelling to Develop People and Organizations* by Margaret Parkin (Kogan Page Limited). Parkin talks about the link between storytelling and the concept of change and transition.

10. *Stories Trainers Tell: 55 Ready-to-Use Stories to Make Training Stick* by Mary B. Wacker and Lori L. Silverman (Jossey-Bass). This book captures thought-provoking stories contributed by trainers, nationally known speakers, consultants, business leaders, educators, and professional storytellers that help make challenging ideas and abstract concepts stick.

11. "It's All in the Delivery" by Assaf Keden, *Communication World* 22, no. 2 (March/April 2005): 14. The article focuses on the relationship between style and substance in employee communication.

12. *The New Yorker Book of Business Cartoons* (Bloomberg Press). A great selection of some of the funniest business cartoons published in *The New Yorker* over the years.

13. "The Chairman and the CFO" by Stanley Bing, *Fortune*, April 18, 2005, 410. This is a funny poem based on Lewis Carroll's "The Walrus and the Carpenter."

Rob DeFlorio is a partner at Mother, New York, the U.S. office of the famous Mother advertising agency in London. I first met Rob when he was at Nike and I was publishing magazines, and I've always loved his energy. He left his job as Global Advertising Director with Nike in 2002 and had just helped open the New York Mother office when I visited him. When I arrived at Rob's office, the elevator door opened to reveal a loft space with just one table. That's right; everybody was sitting at one table — all 30 of them! When Rob told me that the table was core to Mother's philosophy and that the London office had 100 people sitting at the same table, I was blown away. As he explained it further, I started to understand that the table was really a metaphor for open communication, dialogue, connectivity, and equality.

While sitting at one table might be impossible for your team or your company, it's the idea behind the table that is important to think about. How do you promote creativity, support connectivity, and keep people on the same page in this quickly evolving world? One way is to sit together at the same table. But there are other things that can help you achieve some of the same goals — without trying to sell the radical table idea to your boss. Rob's message is clear: Create an environment where communication can thrive, and co-creation and innovative thinking will follow.

Inspiration

When I was the head of advertising for Nike, friends would ask me what I did. I would tell them that my job was to develop and support an environment where creativity could thrive for my team. If that meant building walls around them so they could work, or helping to translate some of the corporate bureaucracy, that's what I did. It also meant helping them break down complex issues into more simple problems to solve. At times, just keeping the timelines, politics, and bullshit at bay so people could continue to think clearly was my main goal.

Create the Right Environment

Now I play the same role at Mother. It's about creating an environment where creativity can thrive. The Mother office in London started this idea of supporting creativity by facilitating better communication. One of the ways they encouraged this was by having a single table where everyone sat. Like many innovations, who knows if it was some brilliant idea that someone thought up theoretically or a more functional thing – I tend to think it was the latter.

Mother started the single table because there was not a lot of money. Eventually, when more people started working there, they just got another table, and then another. It's kind of the way a family might handle growth at home.

When I first walked into the original London office, it was pandemonium! There was literally one big long table where everyone worked. There must have been 60 people sitting at the table. They all had wireless laptops and were all in their little spaces. In both New York and London, everybody has a two-drawer rolling file cabinet, because every three months you're required to move. You certainly don't accumulate a lot more than what you have in your rolling cabinet, otherwise moving is a pain in the ass.

Dealing with Distractions

There are one or two people in charge of the rotation schedule, and neither is a partner in the company. There is really no choice where someone goes. Everyone gets mixed up. Partners sit next to the finance person, who sits next to the copywriter, who sits next to the print production person, and so on. It takes a while to get used to. When I first walked into the London office, I thought, "How the hell do these people work?"

As we did this interview, in fact, there was someone sitting to my left on a conference call – I heard him, he heard me. As we spoke, my finance director was sitting to my right, working on something. I didn't know if he was listening to me or if he even knew I referenced him. What I've realized is that you get used to the noise. Noises cancel each other out.

It's about creating an environment where creativity can thrive.

The table philosophy is interesting in that it fosters immediate communication. Likewise, it also fosters immediate interruption; it creates a culture of interruption. You can be engaged in a conversation with one person and someone else will just interrupt you right in the middle of it. That person doesn't even know he or she is interrupting you. There is an absolute connectivity to everything. It can sometimes be frustrating, but I still think the positives outweigh the negatives.

See the Whole

> There is an absolute connectivity to everything.

In a larger, philosophical sense, when things go wrong in most companies or departments, it's usually because people start thinking that only one thing is their job, like making a rivet. When you sit at one table, you always see the whole picture. You're not just making a rivet; you're making the whole airplane. The environment fosters connectivity and a better understanding of the bigger picture, because you're all in it together and can all see what's happening.

In London, the office moved into a new space where the first level has a staircase, and when you walk up to the second floor, you're physically standing on the table. You can keep walking onto people's workspaces, so you have to actually step down to the floor. I know it sounds crazy, but they like it; it works for them. The reality is, we must keep the connectivity. We look at it like an electrical circuit. There is electricity going through the table. While ungrounded, uninsulated electricity is dangerous, when focused correctly, insulated correctly, and directed correctly, it becomes incredibly useful.

When we opened New York, our architect told us, "You'll never be able to pull this off. It will be too distracting." For the first month, it was. But pretty soon people stopped getting so distracted when someone came up the elevator, for instance. Now we're having a debate about moving to another floor. Our architect is adamant that we can't break up the table. He's gone from saying the idea was insane to being its biggest advocate. He has become a keeper of the flame.

> When you sit at one table, you always see the whole picture.

The Generation Gap

It's amazing when a new employee with a fresh perspective walks in the door. The older, established businesspeople say, "Are you kidding me?" and the younger people think, "Cool." Literally, it doesn't even faze them. They're used to common space. It's amazing to me when I look at the Starbucks culture in New York City. Large living room spaces are scarce, so people tend to view Starbucks as their own living room. They've got their computers and they're sitting there drinking coffee and working. Everyone's multitasking, with their cell phones going and their books spread out. They're living life and adapting to their environment. It's pretty cool. The people who grew up with Starbucks as their living room come to Mother and dig it here. It's no different for them. These same folks are really good at creating their own work environment. They walk into the office,

immediately pull up a chair, sit down, plug in a computer, and put on a headset. They create their own space wherever they are.

The Power of Sharing

The table philosophy seems to play to these employees' strengths. When you come into the office, everyone is on a Mac with an iPod connected, sharing music references. Music gets passed around here really freely. Music infuses creativity at Mother. I'm not trying to be a salesman for Apple here, but there is an ease of use and compatibility designed into these electronic gadgets – people are constantly flipping stuff back and forth. They do the same thing with ideas.

Focus on Innovative Relationships

If any company is interested in improving communication, the table philosophy is worth checking out. Another concept at Mother that's very interesting is that instead of creating a company with multiple departments, this is a company with multiple companies around it. The London Mother team said: "Okay, the design group is going to be its own company with its own name. We are going to have either a controlling stake or a significant minority stake in that company, but then the employees own the rest. They may be on another floor; they may be sitting at the table. They're working for themselves and they're part of a bigger thing – they get salaries, but with the success of the business they have long-term ownership and short-term dividends."

We're starting to do that in the New York office as well. Another advantage of having separate companies, even though they're affiliated and partially

People are constantly flipping stuff back and forth. They do the same thing with ideas.

owned, is that it's a lot easier for that company to do work for you but also have a few of its own clients. Certainly a holding company with multiple companies under it is not new, but small companies operating independently within a larger organization seems like a fresh idea that works for us.

Evolve Your Philosophy

We're not trying to claim that these ideas in themselves are innovative. There are versions of this all over the place. We feel that it's the alchemy of different ideas that's important. It works for our company and our culture. The guys in London started this thing with really basic values, ethics, and ways they like to do business. The four partners in the U.S. got together with them and said, "We're going to carry some of those forward but with our own interpretation."

> I think it's the alchemy of different ideas that's important.

Another interesting thing is that the five partners in Mother's London office were adamant about starting it with people who had never worked for the company before. Almost every other company that expands to a new place tries to export its culture or tether it somehow. These companies always send at least one person to start the office and then hire other locals, trying to keep the gospel going. Instead, the guys from Mother London looked for people they

believed shared the same values. They felt that finding the right people to join them would give their office in New York the ability to carry the vision forward in a unique way. The team in New York has taken the Mother philosophy and applied it in its own ways. I think that has strengthened Mother as a whole with its diversity of thought, skill, and talent.

Let People Interpret the World

That's the Mother philosophy. Take our philosophy and go out into the world, interpreting what you find. The Mother London partners are all British. They know that the American market is very different, and they wanted people who were really familiar with that market. This philosophy is bearing fruit. I give my partners in London a ton of credit. They took the time to find the right people with good ideas. It's difficult when you create something that's your baby and then let it "go out into the world." It took courage for them to let other people take their name and their concept and express it their own way.

In fact, most of the calls we get from London remind me of calls from my parents when I was in college. They ask how we're doing, if we're happy, and whether we need anything. We almost never talk about the financials. The financial conversations are

Take our philosophy and go out into the world, interpreting what you find.

usually just making sure that we're setting the right premiums to reflect our work's worth. They remind us not to sell ourselves short.

Think About Intellectual Diversity

The last thought I'll leave you with is that intellectual diversity is something Mother is superconscious of. The mission for this place is not to be an advertising agency – not to be any kind of business that's already been defined. We want to be a creative cultural center. We're trying to find different ways to have a really interesting, creative mix of people. But we still do need functions and people who do jobs, not just a wonderful little potpourri of interesting, creative people that doesn't make any money.

We want to be a kind of creative magnet with different people bringing different ideas to the party. And interestingly and delightfully, especially for me as a more jaded business guy, our clients perceive us that way. We have a few really large companies that have other resources, more conventional resources, who've hired us to do some of the more unconventional stuff. My theory on this is that if you want to be unconventional and act unconventionally, let someone else label you; don't label yourself or try to be cool. The coolest people are the ones who would never want to be cool. Someone else has to call you that.

> We're trying to find different ways to have a really interesting, creative mix of people.

Tools

❶ **Develop the Right Environment** – If you are a manager, the hardest task is trying to create the right environment for the right work to get done. Sometimes it's the physical environment; other times it's the mental environment. Get your team together and talk about what can change in the environment to make the work more interesting.

❷ **Support Creativity** – Creativity is such a squishy, personal thing. What motivates one person might demotivate another. Support creativity by understanding the creative needs of each of your team members, all the while bringing an understanding of the overall objective.

❸ **Knock Down the Walls** – Knock down some walls and see what happens. Hey, have everybody sit at the same table! Promote a more open environment. Sure, there might be more distractions, but there will be more communication as well.

❹ **Facilitate Better Communication** – What can you do to facilitate better communication? Try putting up visual cues of the projects you are working on. Can you take an office, small conference room, or even an empty cube and build a creative space for communication? Take everyone out to lunch once a month. Get to know your team members better as people.

❺ **Focus on Connectivity** – I was shocked how dramatically our office changed when we installed a wireless network. People would carry their computers everywhere. Every meeting benefited from having necessary information at everyone's fingertips. Think about other ways to stay more connected. Can people move as they work on different projects with different people? The key to connectivity is flexibility.

❻ Understand That Everyone Works Differently – Think about the individuals on your team. What are their backgrounds? Are they used to a more traditional, private office space? Or are they part of the Starbucks generation and more used to the interruption model of working in a disruptive environment? Facilitate being more innovative by creating the right kind of environment for different team members.

❼ Hire More Outsiders – Think about shaking up your team a bit by bringing in someone from the outside for a day, week, or month – maybe even permanently. Think about the existing chemistry on your team. Are they really co-creating innovation together? If not, throw some new energy into the mix.

❽ Encourage Intellectual Diversity – Can you get someone from elsewhere in the company to join your team for a bit? It might only be a meeting or two. Try to create an environment where there is intellectual diversity. When recruiting new people to your team, think about hiring someone different. Find someone who will be a good team player but also will challenge the status quo.

❾ Be a Creative Magnet – If you make it, they will come. If you create a fun environment for you and your team and have a diverse group of talented people co-creating innovative solutions, then you will have the most talented people banging on your door to work with you.

_____

_____

_____

_____

_____

_____

_____

_____

_____

_____

_____

_____

_____

_____

_____

_____

Communicate Faster

Think about how you can take the table philosophy and morph it into something appropriate for your environment. Draw a diagram of how you might rearrange your team's space to maximize creativity and communications.

Communicate Faster

Resources

1. **"Experiences in the Use of a Media Space,"** *Groupware: Software for Computer-Supported Cooperative Work* by M. M. Mantei, R. M. Baecker, A. J. Sellen, W. A. S. Buxton, T. Milligan, and B. Wellman, IEEE Computer Society Press: http://www.chass.utoronto.ca/~wellman/publications/mediaspace/experiences.pdf. Explores a system that uses integrated video, audio, and computers and allows individuals and groups to work together despite being distributed spatially and temporally.

2. **"Introducing Instant Messaging and Chat in the Workplace"** by J. D. Herbsleb, D. L. Atkins, D. G. Boyer, M. Handel, and T. A. Finholt, Conference on Human Factors in Computing Systems, Minneapolis, MN: http://www.cs.uoregon.edu/~datkins/papers/chi-rvm.pdf. The authors report on their experiences of introducing an instant messaging and group chat application into geographically distributed workgroups.

3. **"Interaction and Outeraction: Instant Messaging in Action"** by B. A. Nardi, S. Whittaker, and E. Bradner, CSCW, December 2–6, 2000, Philadelphia, PA: http://dis.shef.ac.uk/stevewhittaker/outeraction_cscw2000.pdf. This paper features the results from an ethnographic study of instant messaging in the workplace and its implications.

4. *The New Office* by Francis Duffy (Conran-Octopus). Duffy offers a good exploration of new ways to work.

5. *The Great Good Place: Cafés, Coffee Shops, Bookstores, Bars, Hair Salons, and Other Hangouts at the Heart of a Community* by R. Oldenburg (Marlowe). Oldenburg argues that "third places" – where people can gather – are the heart of a community's social vitality and the grassroots of democracy.

6. *Communities of Practice: Learning, Meaning & Identity* by E. Wegner (Cambridge). Wegner presents a framework for learning as part of people's responsibility at work, at home, at school.

7. "Designs for Working: Why Your Bosses Want to Turn Your New Office into Greenwich Village" by M. Gladwell, *The New Yorker,* December 11, 2000. Gladwell explores how cutting-edge office design has its roots in bustling urban mixtures of work, life, and commerce, like Greenwich Village during the 1950s.

8. *The 21st Century Office: Architecture and Design for the New Millennium* by J. Myerson and P. Ross (Rizzoli). This is a comprehensive survey of workplace architecture and emerging themes and ideas in office design from around the world.

9. *The Inspired Workspace: Interior Designs for Creativity & Productivity* by M. Zelinsky (Rockport). Zelinsky explores the creative souls of more than 40 successful firms.

10. "The New Culture Czars" by Tyler Cowen, *Forbes*, April 19, 2004. Explores how companies are becoming the new cultural creators.

11. "Corporate Governance, Communication, and Getting Social Values into the Decisional Chain" by Stanley Deetz, *Management Communication Quarterly* 16, no. 4 (May 2003). Deetz provides a good discussion on corporate governance, communication, and getting social values into the decisional chain of organizations.

I first met Matt Jacobson at the height of the dot-com craziness. He was running the Internet business for Fox Broadcasting and was in the center of all the action. After working at both Fox and Disney, Matt really understands how media can make a difference in connecting with customers in a powerful way.

Today, as the vice president of Quiksilver Entertainment, part of the $1 billion action sports apparel brand, Matt's work gives him the opportunity to help grow the action sports marketplace. Quiksilver is a giant in the industry, several magnitudes larger than most of its competitors. The combination of Quiksilver's size relative to the market and its desire to work with competitors to grow the market through the use of media induced me to include Matt's story.

Matt's perspective on benevolent leadership, being balanced, keeping things small, and letting go all add a lot to the concepts of co-creation and innovation. As Matt says, "It's a kind of holistic approach to the way we do business – I think the era of bullies and assholes is over." I also believe that we are entering a new era of business in which companies will gain from being less competitive and more inclusive and by building deeper relationships with suppliers, customers, and, yes, even competitors. Many of the industries I have worked in are more threatened by other industries gaining momentum than by competitors in the market. Remember the saying, "A high tide floats all boats"? In exploring new types of relationships, being more connected and building co-creation among your team, think of media as an important tool to form a foundation for innovation. Whether it's distributing videos or publishing books, like Quiksilver, or producing blogs, like Stonyfield Farm (Chapter 16), media will both contribute to and enhance your business relationships.

Something that I really care about is the whole concept of what we call "benevolent market leadership" – for us that means doing things that grow the overall market for action sports. I mean, we're a really big fish in a medium-size pond. So the question for us is, How do we do things to grow the pond? That's really what we're looking at; that's what all this is about. Whether it's *Surf Girls* on MTV or the Luna Bay Book series or our latest book, *Have Board, Will Travel*, it's getting our story out of the monastery to a bigger audience. And we're happy to compete on a level playing field or just on a bigger field.

Grow the Market

Danny Kwok and I founded Quiksilver Entertainment four years ago. We put together a business plan with the mission to do two things – one, be profitable, and two, grow the overall market for action sports in an authentic way. I think everybody saw what other action sports companies had done – you know, creating an entertainment division and original programming around a lifestyle. It's great in concept, but it's fiendishly complicated to pull off. I think that everybody from Polo to Tommy has tried to do it in joint ventures with NBC. But what those companies attempted was really about their own brand and not about the overall market.

I think the fact that we've stayed really true to this vision of doing things that support and expand the market as a whole is powerful – more so than trying to do it on our own – and I think that's the most critical part. What happens is that the people in our company embrace the vision and have something to be proud of – they don't need to be defensive about the business when they talk to the industry at large, because generally what we've done is what we've said we were going to do.

> We've stayed really true to this vision of doing things that support and expand the market as a whole.

Leverage Media Yourself

It's incredible when you start getting orders of a magnitude greater than your competitors. There are things that are incumbent on you to do as a market leader because if you don't, no one else will. That's what led to the development of Union, the mainstream video distribution business we started. It's an industrywide initiative, and the opportunity was that we were all producing videos and it was no secret what it cost to

make them. They're expensive, and we're limited in distribution because of the size of the search gate and snow market.

We won't distribute just anything – we go looking for something that generally has a narrative – that isn't just a video magazine, right? These are titles that have some importance in the category. We pulled together 150 hours of material from all sources – independent filmmakers and other action sports companies – and we said, "Somebody needs to do this." Now, we have great movies, and we need to get them distributed as mainstream and bring them together as a common brand, because otherwise they'll be put on a special-interest shelf somewhere and won't amount to anything.

We decided to create a new brand – Union – as an entity to distribute these titles and see if we could make it work. That's what we've been doing for the past couple of years. Danny and I were passionate about it and made a good case for it and didn't announce anything until we had a couple of deals. Once we had the deals, we said, "Okay, let's go for it," and everybody supported it.

Be Involved Everywhere

I think doing this kind of marketing or branding, because it's nonspecific to the company, can be applied to any business. I've had this discussion before with soft-drink and beer brands about how hard it is to increase, say, the number of university students who are thirsty, their market. I think it would work for automakers as well as motorcycle companies. In fact, many industries could do it, but they may not be inclined to think that way. It could happen with a

> I think doing this kind of marketing or branding, being nonspecific to the company, can be applied to any business.

specific technology, as it did with the digital distribution of media.

There could be a better way than trying to divide and conquer; there could be a consortium dedicated to digital distribution and media. Take Intel, for example. Intel was the model for us when we put this business together: "Let's be the 'Intel inside.' Let's do the ingredient brand." Intel was happy to support everybody in the PC industry because it had a 90 percent chance that these products were going to contain Intel silicon. Dolby did the same thing with its Dolby trademark. Those two companies were our muses for how to shape Union.

> There could be better ways than trying to divide and conquer.

Find Balance

Before all this started, I was at Disney for 4 years and NewsCorp for almost 13 years, and then I went to Broadcom; I worked in the semiconductor space before coming to Quiksilver. One of the things that has been great for me – one of the things that's really great about this company – is the emphasis on balance. There's a theory that corporate America is changing, one company at a time, and what is important to people now is different from what was important to people 15 or 20 years ago. Whereas before it was about power, prestige, and money, now people who, I

think, are savvy and have a good head on their shoulders are really much more concerned about balance – the balance of lifestyle.

The equilibrium between life and lifestyle – or work and lifestyle – is what our company is really about. I've become a much more centered, balanced person because I've been able to pursue something I believe in. It's a kind of holistic approach to the way we do business – I think the era of bullies and assholes is over. By finding partners we like to work with, we sort of put all of our wood behind a couple of arrows, so to speak. Those are the people we want to work with and the way we want to work for companies. That kind of fluidity to pick and choose our partners and our projects makes for a healthier company and healthier people.

Keep It Small

Another one of our goals is to always keep it small. The business started with Danny, an assistant, and me. Then we brought in a business development person and promoted our assistant to a development job, and we had an intern who became our in-house producer. Danny and I are still superintegrated in the whole operation I really believe that we're good partners. I like to go into meetings and tell people that we're good partners – we're not stupid, we're not pushovers, we're just good partners. I think we have an interesting company, and it's really well run with a great leader. I love that we take very pure information streams from people we trust and empower those people to make decisions. We are very open and flexible to the dynamic of making it up every day.

> I like that we take very pure information streams from people that we trust and empower those people to make decisions.

Back People You Believe In

A year and a half ago, when the women's surf business was supposed to be flat, *Surf Girls* was running 120 times or more on MTV for 54 million viewers, and our Roxy business was up 12 percent across the board. I think that speaks to educating people about this market. We had people calling and e-mailing to say that they didn't know there was a difference between short and long boarding or wanting to know where to get those glasses or that swimwear or wet suit. I appreciate that we can be involved as owners, who are not just concerned about checkbook marketing but also about how to really make a difference. We can option books that we believe in, and we're producing movies and backing people we believe in.

> You feel motivated and empowered, like you're making a difference.

Make a Difference

I think you need to let some things go – all the inner demons, like being competitive and hating your competitors and always looking over your shoulder to wipe them out before they can eliminate you. Let go of that kind of thinking and instead say, "Listen, there's an opportunity here." Maybe that doesn't matter if you're a complete monopoly – like say Wrigley's Gum – and don't need to grow the market for your product. But I'll tell you, if you want to live a better, more balanced life, I highly recommend this way because you'll definitely feel better when you get up in the morning. You'll feel motivated and empowered, like you're making a difference instead of just focusing on who you're going to try to take out that day.

Follow Your Intuition

❶ Focus on Benevolent Leadership – Every company can be more benevolent to people, both internally and externally. Maybe your company isn't. Matt talks about it from the perspective of a market leader. But what would happen if you were more thoughtful and benevolent when dealing with your customers or suppliers?

❷ Focus on Customer Needs, Not Your Wants – So many of us think about innovation from the perspective of evolving our own products, whether there is a need in the marketplace or not. Instead of seeing innovation only from your perspective, think about how your product or service might better meet a customer's needs.

❸ Use Media to Leverage Your Cause – Quiksilver has gotten involved in media in an interesting way, helping to grow the market by bringing more attention to action sports. What can you do to grow the pie? Start a blog. Write a letter to an editor of a magazine. Get involved with an industry organization.

❹ Be Balanced – There seems to be a new spirit emerging in business, one that focuses on the power of relationships and putting cooperation over competition. Can you work with another company as partners to develop a breakthrough innovation? Can you find a new, balanced approach to working with others in your industry for the benefit of all? Likewise, can you work with competitive divisions within your company in a more balanced way?

❺ Be More Holistic – Bring a more holistic perspective to your work. Invite people from other parts of your company to your team's meetings. Get their perspective on your project. Try to get a better idea of how all of the pieces fit together in an environment.

❻ Be More Fluid and Dynamic – Change is hard. Yet sometimes change is all you have to hold on to. How can you make your team more fluid and dynamic? Can you use technology to leverage co-creation?

❼ Do More with Less – Cut your resources, and I'll bet you can do more. Smaller teams working on an innovation issue can often move faster and be less threatening to the rest of the company. By working with fewer resources, you have to co-create solutions with others in the company, finding internal and accessible supporters and mentors.

❽ Let Go – Try letting go of some of your tightly held beliefs about your capabilities, your team members, and your customers. We all hold on to things that are only our perceptions of a situation. Try focusing on bringing a beginner's mind to your work. How does this fresh perspective change your attitude?

_____

_____

_____

_____

_____

_____

_____

_____

_____

_____

_____

_____

_____

_____

Follow Your Intuition

Think about ways for your team to be a benevolent leader for the company and even the market while working on an innovation problem. Can you bring more balance to the team by being more transparent, inviting co-creation?

Follow Your Intuition

1. Quiksilver's Web site: http://www.quiksilver.com.

2. "Tribal Marketing: The Tribalisation of Society and its Impact on the Conduct of Marketing" by B. Cova and V. Cova, *European Journal of Marketing* 36, nos. 5-6 (June 2002): 595-620. The authors explore the power of community and the need to change the marketing model from individual to tribal.

3. "Cosmic Profit: Countercultural Commerce and the Problem of Trust in American Marketing" by Sam Binkley, *Consumption, Markets and Culture* 6 (December 2003): 231–49. This article focuses on the demise of impersonal mass marketing and its replacement by lifestyle marketing.

4. *Lifestyle Marketing: Reaching the New American Consumer* by R. D. Michman, E. M. Mazze, and A. J. Greco (Praeger). This book offers a good overview of how the proliferation of lifestyles has influenced sales and marketing strategies.

5. "Company Culture Provides Competitive Edge for Sargento Foods" by B. Gannon and J. Sterling, *Strategy and Leadership* 32 (March 2004): 31-35. The authors look at the Wisconsin-based cheese processing and marketing company Sargento Foods and how people and culture have become a core element of corporate strategy.

6. "The Citizen-Consumer: Media Effects at the Intersection of Consumer and Civic Culture" by H. Keum, D. Narayan, S. Deshpande, M. R. Nelson, and D. V. Shah, *Political Communication* 21, no. 3 (July-September 2004). The authors explore the replacement of civic culture with consumer culture.

7. "Storytelling: Transferring Tacit Corporate Knowledge in Different Cultures" by Parissa Haghirian and Tina C. Chini: http://www.sses.com/public/events/euram/complete_tracks/management_play/haghirian_chini.pdf. This article explores the use of storytelling as a tool for the transfer of tacit knowledge within organizations.

8. "Corporate Art or Artful Corporation? The Emerging Philosophy Firm" by Pierre Guillet de Monthoux and Sven-Erik Sjöstrand: http://www.sses.com/public/events/euram/complete_tracks/management_play/monthoux_sjostrand.pdf. The article discusses how art and artistic principles have entered the discourses and practices of modern managers and corporations.

9. "Caught in the Iron Cage of Creativity – The Ten Commandments of the Creative Field" by Daniel Ericsson: http://www.sses.com/public/events/euram/complete_tracks/management_play/ericsson.pdf. The author looks at the concept of creativity and why it has become so prominent among managers today.

10. The X Games home page: http://expn.go.com/expn/index.

11. *The Five Patterns of Extraordinary Careers: The Guide for Achieving Success and Satisfaction* by James M. Citrin and Richard A. Smith (Crown Business). This is a good exploration of benevolent leadership.

12. "Action Sports Success: Total Immersion Required" by Kathleen DesMarteau, *Apparel Magazine* 45, no. 10 (June 2004): 12. DesMarteau takes a look inside the skateboarding industry and provides a compelling example of lifestyle marketing at its best.

13. "Lights, Camera, ACTION SPORTS!" by Barry Janoff, *Brandweek*, February 28, 2005, 26. Janoff looks at the use of extreme sports in the advertising campaigns of companies in the U.S.

14. "Marketing to Lifestyles: Action Sports and Generation Y" by Gregg Bennett and Tony Lachowetz, *Sport Marketing Quarterly* 13, no. 4:239. The authors discuss the power of the action sports genre to the Generation Y market.

When I met Jeff Garwood, new product development manager at Miller Brewing Company, I thought to myself, Here's a great guy! He's thoughtful, sensitive, and inquisitive; he also fits the beer business like a glove.

Two things that really fascinate me about Jeff are his quest for learning and the way he values good experiences over the sole focus of accomplishments. Jeff seems to have such a nice balance. This quest for experience has taken him to a half-dozen different jobs in different departments within Miller in the past 16 years. Jeff has a great understanding about how the whole company works and has gained a great deal of respect from different departments because he has the credibility of being "one of them." While this might not work for everyone or every company, it does highlight the importance of putting together a diverse team, one that can get others in the organization to support you and your project.

Jeff also has a nice balance between his life and his work that gives him the ability to refuel, bring new creativity to the table, and have the energy to see things through. We can all take a few notes about giving attention to other parts of our lives – at least I know I can – and gain the added benefit of having a fresh perspective.

Inspiration

When I started out with Miller 16 years ago, I was right out of college and rejoicing at my good fortune: "I'm going to work for a beer company…I cannot be happier!" But once I started working at Miller, I quickly recognized that there was so much to the business I wanted to learn – not that I *had* to learn but that I just *wanted* to learn because I was curious. I would always look for and accept new responsibilities, as long as the experiences kept me learning more and more about the business.

Be a Generalist

I was in a quality assurance role for packaging for about a year, and then I went to another brewery where I was in a product quality assurance role. I learned almost everything about the brewing process. When I came up to purchasing, I started getting the business background from another standpoint. My curiosity led me to ask the question, What happens after the brewery? Well, there was marketing and sales, so I moved into a marketing services role.

Probably about halfway through, I realized I was happiest when I was learning about the business in generalist terms. I never wanted to be a packaging innovation specialist, even though that is what I am. My strength is that I know almost the entire business as well as anyone else in the company. I have a desire to keep learning as a generalist, to go a mile wide and an inch deep across the whole organization and understand the needs and wants and thinking of everybody.

So how do I keep it fresh? How do I maintain motivation? I'm always learning something new about the business, and there are still aspects about the business that I don't know well enough for myself, in particular sales and distribution.

Keep Things in Perspective

From the standpoint of getting out of the day-to-day routine and out of the rut – that's hard. I also bring an extreme balance to my work in a couple of ways. My work is not all consuming – I make it a priority to spend time with my family and also have personal time so that I can separate myself from work and go home or do things outside of work. I coach some of my kids' sports teams, ride my Harley, and enjoy

I would always look for and accept new responsibilities, as long as it kept me learning more and more about the business.

walking to get coffee on the weekends. I think that all helps me manage stress, but it also clears my mind and allows me to be a more creative thinker.

There are other things I do to stay fresh and keep motivated, such as continually looking outside the business for ideas that are beyond what I currently know. I'm an avid reader and not necessarily of just marketing books or other business-related publications. I'm also reading fiction. I love to read and I think that helps with creativity and motivation and keeps my mind fresh. As far as getting out – well, we have focus groups and such, but we've seldom been in consumers' homes or gone shopping with them. I read a lot of material that our research generates for us, but it's not the same. I get a totally different angle when I go out, take myself out of my current surroundings, and go to the customer's or consumer's surroundings. That's the other component of getting out – having the intent of gaining insights or of learning something new or getting a small, or a big, "Aha!"

> There are other things that I do to stay fresh and keep motivated, such as continually looking outside the business for ideas.

Focus on Learning

I also have to look at what makes me happy, and learning about the business – the total business versus one functional area – energizes me, motivates me, makes

me happy. I mean, I could have had a fast-track career path in procurement, but it wasn't for me. I wouldn't have been happy there long term. And then I would have ended up leaving Miller Brewing Company to work in other procurement departments trying to better my financial standing instead of bettering myself as a person and as a contributor to increasing value at Miller.

Maybe I'm a unique individual. Then again, I think I'm the right type of individual to be in an innovation role, because I'm used to change, used to challenges, used to frustration, and not so worried about a leadership career path – unless it's one where I can continually challenge myself and learn about the business. Financial position and the like are very important to the security of my family and me, but I do have security with Miller, and I think I'm the luckiest guy there because I get to work across the whole company.

> I think I'm the luckiest guy at Miller, because I get to work across the whole company.

Be a Teacher

I often have the opportunity to meet with interns on the marketing side, and sometimes I work with them. The new hires that come in are usually sent over to talk to me too. I talk to them more about doing business within Miller than about their career. I tell them they need to focus on their role and their function within their work group or team, but there's a bigger picture, and they should not assume they know what it is. It's better to get out and learn about it, even if it's on your own time.

Whether your career path is within procurement or operations, if you understand the marketing and sales and distribution roles as a generalist, it will

make you a better employee. You'll understand the decisions that are forced on you in some instances, or you'll be able to ask good questions about some of the decisions that are being considered. My advice is to learn about the business. Don't assume that a purchasing role is just about buying things; there's an innovation component and there's a marketing component that you have to be aware of so you can make the best decisions for your department and organization.

Get out there and learn about it, even if it's on your own time.

Focus on a Variety of Roles

I feel like I've gained a tremendous amount of credibility by working throughout the company, in particular from groups I haven't worked specifically with. I haven't had a sales role, but I've worked hand in hand with sales and have a lot of credibility there because they understand I've worked across the company. They know my insights aren't just whims but are based on a tremendous amount of knowledge that I've accrued over 16 years.

While much of my knowledge comes from working at a larger company, I think it should be even easier in a smaller company to learn about the business. The one thing I think we do well at Miller from a big-business standpoint is to make fact-based decisions. We probably gather too much information; we're a big company and can be guilty of paralysis by analysis. But I think a small company could learn from Miller to gather as much information as it needs before making a decision. At a smaller company, it's probably easier to have more influence with a generalist idea of the overall business.

Style Is Important

I have learned that in some situations within different groups, it's important to manage my way of addressing their specific areas of knowledge. For instance, in the quality assurance and procurement group, I have to be careful not to direct people. I don't necessarily want to come across as the guy who says, "This is what I want you to do." I want to drive debate and conversation, but I do have to be cognizant of not stepping on other groups' roles and responsibilities. On the other hand, they are often more willing to let me direct or make purchasing decisions on development projects because they're sometimes overwhelmed. I embrace that, but I couldn't in a vacuum. I still have to engage people. By doing that, they become more involved and supportive of my direction.

> I still have to engage people. By doing that, they become more involved and supportive of my direction.

Just recently, I started coaching my son's basketball team, and even though I played basketball a little in high school and know the basics, it was a challenge. I was challenging myself to be a good coach to 6- and 7-year-old kids, to make basketball fun for them while still teaching them some basics. It was also a personal challenge because I needed to make sure I understood how to coach kids and at the same time teach them and make it fun.

I guess for me it's the learning, the applying of knowledge or experience, summed up by always trying to be better at what I do. I strive to be a generalist in all things. I have cleaned pools, worked at McDonald's in high school, and worked in a gym as a trainer in college. My first role at Miller was as a packaging analyst – my first purchasing role – then buyer and senior buyer in purchasing. From there, I became packaging innovation manager, senior manager of brand identity and packaging development, and currently project manager in new product development (although that title probably needs to have packaging innovation put back into it). And even though I did study marketing eventually, my undergraduate degree was in biology.

> I guess for me it's the learning, applying of knowledge or experience aspect, summed up by just always trying to get better.

Variety Is Key

I talk about family a lot, and I'm going to use my son as an example here. I'm from a sports family. My father was a football coach, and I was expected to play football, which I did in college. But I don't care if my son ever plays football. I do want him to have athletic experiences. I want him to try soccer, basketball, baseball, skiing, snowboarding, and golf – get a variety

of exposure and experience. Do as much as you can, and then down the road you can make the decisions that allow you to pick what makes you happy – you'll have that exposure. You'll have a broader spectrum to choose from and say, "You know, this really makes me happy, and this is what I choose to do."

Break Out of Your Routine

❶ Focus on Learning – Instead of always considering ways to advance your career, focus on learning. Volunteer for interesting projects. Try to connect with people both inside and outside the company who can help you learn. This might be a customer or someone from a different department with whom you're not in close contact.

❷ Experiences versus Accomplishment – We all get obsessed with trying to get things done. Instead, spend some time each day with someone new. Go check out what's happening in other parts of the company. In most companies, there are abundant opportunities for innovation just by connecting two seemingly disconnected dots.

❸ Be a Generalist – Jeff's ability to work in lots of different roles inside Miller has given him the ability to see a broader landscape of the company and garner more respect from others because he understands their perspective. It's easy for all of us to drill ever deeper in our specialty. While sometimes that's needed, pay attention to what else is going on and learn about things that might be tangential to your project.

❹ Keep Work in Perspective – It's easy to obsess over a problem at work and bring it home at night, sequestered in front of the computer answering e-mails while a child or spouse is trying to engage you in a conversation. Put your work away. For most of us, nothing terrible will happen if we don't return an e-mail before morning. By taking a break, you will recharge your capacity for creative thought.

⑤ Go Outside for Inspiration – When you get stuck on a project, as we all do, take a break. Look outside the company for inspiration. Can you go talk to a customer? Visit a retailer and look at competitive products? Maybe it's taking your shoes off and walking around in the grass barefoot. Whatever you do, get outside.

⑥ Read More – As a writer, I'm often overwhelmed by reading. Many days, I just can't read another word. Yet picking up a good book always brings me a fresh perspective. The mind is a muscle. If you want to be more innovative, you've got to feed it and exercise it with innovative thinking and perspectives.

⑦ Keep the Big Picture in Mind – It's easy to get buried in the day-to-day activities of answering e-mails and going to meetings and forget why you're even doing what you're doing. Keep the big picture in mind by creating a collage of images and words that keep you energized and on track with what you're trying to do.

⑧ Apply a Different Perspective – Play the devil's advocate in a meeting. Reverse your roles with a team member. Change the way you think about a problem by thinking about it from a customer's perspective. Remember, your customers don't think about your product 24/7 like you might. How does what you do fit into their lives?

_____

_____

_____

_____

_____

_____

_____

_____

_____

_____

_____

_____

_____

_____

Constantly Break Out of Your Routine

Think about a current innovation challenge. How can you focus part of your energy on learning versus accomplishing? Think about your life. Is there balance between your work and your life? Do you encourage, even tacitly, your employees to work 24/7? How can you facilitate a kind of balance between your work life and your real life that enables you to recharge your batteries regularly? How can you create a balanced environment that is energized and vibrant?

Resources

1. Miller Brewing Company's Web site: http://www.millerbrewing.com.

2. "Why the Microbrewery Movement? Organizational Dynamics of Resource Partitioning in the U.S. Brewing Industry" by G. R. Carroll and A. Swaminathan, *American Journal of Sociology* 106, no. 3 (November 2000): 715. This is an interesting look at the microbrewery business in the U.S.

3. "The Renaissance of Learning in Business" by John Thompson, *Learning Organizations* (New Leaders Press): http://www.acumen.com/pdf/renaissance_learning.pdf. Thompson discusses why corporations' survival in today's business environment increasingly depends on their ability to learn and adapt.

4. "Field Investigation of the Relationship Among Adult Curiosity, Workplace Learning, and Job Performance" by Thomas G. Reio Jr. and Albert Wiswell, *Human Resource Development Quarterly* 11, no. 1:5-30. A good look at curiosity's role in adult learning in the workplace.

5. "E" is for Engagement: Transforming Your Business by Transforming Your People" by James A. Haudan and Donald MacLean, *Journal of Change Management* 2, no. 3 (September 2001). The authors explore the concept of engagement and learning as it applies to change management.

6. "Action with Attitude: Harley-Davidson's Jim Brolley Revs Up Learning" by Kelley Whitney, *Chief Learning Officer* 4, no. 3 (March 2005): 36. Whitney focuses on the effort of Jim Brolley, director of organizational learning and development at Harley-Davidson Inc., to sustain an environment encouraging intellectual curiosity and learning.

7. "The Biology of Joy" by Michael D. Lemonick and Dan Cray, *Time*, January 17, 2005. The authors examine new research into the biology of joy.

8. "How To: Find the Hidden Value" by Duff McDonald, *Business 2.0*, December 2004, 102. An interesting interview with Barry Diller, chairman, InterActive Corp., about how his guiding principle in business is following his own curiosity.

9. "Innovation: The Sum of Curiosity and Discipline" by Art Wittmann, *Network Magazine* 19, no. 11 (November 2004): 11. Wittmann explores the importance of adopting innovations in ensuring the success of a business.

10. "Curiosity and Exploration: Facilitating Positive Subjective Experiences and Personal Growth Opportunities" by Todd B. Kashdan, P. Rose, and Frank D. Fincham, *Journal of Personality Assessment* 82, no. 3 (June 2004): 291. This is an interesting look at curiosity as it relates to personal growth.

11. "Innovate, Or Take a Walk" by Tom Yager, *InfoWorld* 26, no. 16 (April 19, 2004): 69. Yager takes a look at innovation in the information technology business and how it relates to outsourcing.

12. "Balanced Skills and Entrepreneurship" by Edward Lazear, *American Economic Review* 94, no. 2 (May 2004): 208. Lazear explores the view that entrepreneurs are generalists who are good at a variety of skills although not necessarily excellent at any one.

13. "How to Kill Creativity" by T. M. Amabile, *Harvard Business Review*, Sept.-Oct. 1998:76-87, 186. In the pursuit of productivity, efficiency, and control, it's easy for businesses to undermine creativity.

The Company

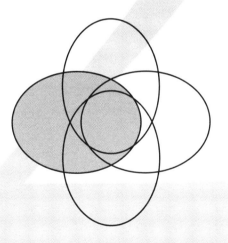

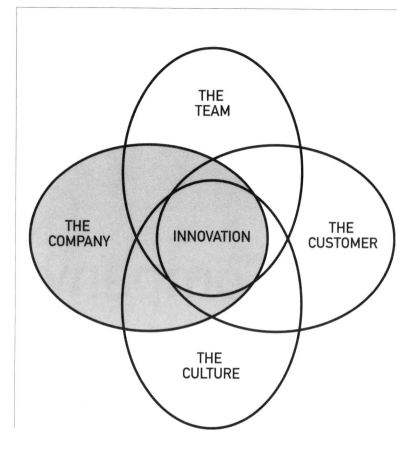

THE TEAM

THE COMPANY

INNOVATION

THE CUSTOMER

THE CULTURE

F or any real innovation to be co-created, all the members of a company must have a shared framework and a common understanding of the innovation problem to be solved. Sometimes, however, a company's internal culture gets in the way of creating this shared meaning. All companies have their own filters and assumptions that over time harden into mental models of the world. These models can act as a lens, or filter, that alters the way the company sees the world. A company cannot forget its own history. Ironically, many times companies that have been the most successful have the thickest lenses. Their own success has told them that the world works in a specific way. Hence, when the paradigm shifts they may be the last to notice.

The real key to overcoming these issues is to find internal alignment or understanding around an innovation opportunity and have a flexible system of co-creating innovation. The four chapters in this section, "Create an Innovative Environment," "Space Matters," "Be Brave," and "Maximize Creative Resources," provide a platform for you to understand new ways to develop shared meaning and new dynamism in the way your company approaches innovation. Mark Parker, Henry Beer, Scott Bowers, and Marsha Skidmore will inspire you to think about new ways to find a deeper connection not only to people inside the company but also to people and the culture outside the company.

've known Mark Parker, president of Nike Brand, for a long time and have always marveled at the diversity of his knowledge. He is a true renaissance man who feels equally comfortable cruising the streets of Tokyo, checking out the underground art scene, or working with professional athletes to divine the future of a sport. What impresses me most, however, is his ability to identify and support other creative and innovative people. He really has a sixth sense when it comes to innovation.

Many companies struggling with sporadic innovation have great people who know how to innovate yet who suffer from a lack of support from senior management in making innovation a priority. Mark's ideas regarding learning from failure, reducing bureaucracy, encouraging communication, and not getting stuck using only one method are all important in an effort to support the co-creation of innovation. Such a management style is critical for the success of any innovative company in today's uncertain business and cultural environment. Too often, annual reports profess the concept that upper management supports innovation, yet those trying to actually innovate are so weighed down by the bureaucracy of counting and tracking that they have no time to co-create new products and services.

Companies that consistently innovate, like Nike, not only talk the innovation talk – they also walk the innovation walk. To innovate today, businesses need to have a deep personal knowledge of their product, market, and customers, combined with ongoing support and the belief in an organic innovation practice.

Nike is a company fixated on innovation. It's what we look for in every idea, every project, and every relationship. We expect it of ourselves and respect it in others. I don't consider it to be a fringe benefit or a lucky byproduct of our business. I consider it to be a prime directive, something I take very personally.

Sports is said to be a metaphor for life; we believe that. This is incredibly important to how we do business. On any day, in any event, at any game, anything can happen. World records snap in the blink of an eye. Vegas odds crumble when one athlete digs deeper than the rest. You have to have talent. You have to put in the hours training. And you have to believe. When you do, you unleash the power of possibility. This is the foundation of inspiration and innovation – the sense of possibility.

Creative Structure

Nike is a big company. We have 25,000 employees spread out across the world. In a sense, Nike is a society. It requires structure and guidelines to operate with any degree of efficiency. I don't consider this a hindrance to innovation but rather a tool to pursue it. Leonardo da Vinci stands alone as a creative thinker, but much of his ability came about through studying the physical aspects of the senses. He was as interested in how the eyes worked as in what they saw. That kind of emphasis on structure can yield incredible gains in the creative process.

We have several organized and established advanced R&D groups. Engineers, developers, researchers, and others who aren't defined as creative in the classic sense of the word are responsible for a lot of divergent thinking. They embrace trial and error – always willing to take risks, to go down different paths and hit some dead ends, back up and regroup. And they learn from it all. That's just the nature of the beast. Much of the innovation at Nike comes from these formal groups. At Nike, leadership and management understand this and support it.

> Often it's about finding the right "chemistry" – not just how **good** people are as individuals but how well they work together.

The Right Chemistry

We also promote a less formal SWAT team approach, especially where speed is critical and a specific mix of individuals can really attack an opportunity. Often

it's about finding the right "chemistry" – not just how good people are as individuals but how well they work together. You may have someone who doesn't have the greatest résumé or experience, but when put on the right team that person creates great energy and incredible things because the chemistry is right.

This approach is very powerful in designing products, but it also happens in other parts of the company – marketing, communications, operations, supply chain, and retail. Great ideas can come from anywhere. True brilliance is rare, but I think creativity in people is the norm and not the exception. The key is the ability to visualize what an idea can be, to elaborate on it, stretch, and poke and play with possibilities that can be brought to life in earnest and not just in theory.

> True brilliance is rare, but I think creativity in people is the norm and not the exception.

Amplify the Focus
Even with all these efforts, you're going to face tough times when things don't work, when the well runs dry. There was a point back in the late '80s when Nike's growth flattened and the company was struggling. So we put together the "Speed Group" to accelerate the design and development of what we

thought were the most compelling product concepts of the time, whatever might be rattling around in our Advanced R&D group. The results included "Visible AIR" technology and "Cross-Training" footwear, two defining moments in our history of innovation. It was a matter of pulling together the best people to work on this particular list of projects and giving them the support and backing they needed to get it done quickly.

Sometimes, you need to work around the larger organization when it starts to sag under its own weight. You look for ways to shake it up, amplify the focus, energize the sense of urgency, get on a mission, get each other excited, and create momentum. Managing this type of "disruption" in the organization can be very delicate. But if you're open and you communicate, people tend to let their guard down and trust a lot more. I found that to be very helpful. In the end, what really matters are results. When people start to see that they're moving fast and producing some really good work and that what they are doing can really help the company in a big way, they start to rally.

> Look for ways to shake it up, amplify the focus, energize the sense of urgency, get on a mission, get each other excited, and create momentum.

The Customer Is the Boss

You also have to be very careful that you don't lose sight of who you're working for. At Nike we all work for one boss – the consumer. Consumers are tough and they're smart, they have choices, they have power, and they like to use it. They understand the world of innovation. They mash together sports and music and film and gaming and art and food and fashion. They ignore the superficial scratch and hiss of brandsters. They are not beyond influence, but they are above manipulation.

Nike succeeds in this world of consumers for some very good reasons. First, we make good products. It doesn't matter how cool you are, you aren't cool for long if you don't stand and deliver. Second, we have the strength of our convictions. We love sports and design. We like to have a good time. And we find great joy in getting off the beaten path. Third, we listen to consumers. We talk to consumers. We ask consumers. And we respond to consumers. That's why they like and trust Nike. As long as we stay connected to them, we'll be able to keep our products innovative and relevant.

We talk to consumers. We ask consumers. And we respond to consumers.

Refuel Yourself

It's very important for me to keep my own sense of possibility and curiosity cranked up. I travel a lot and have the good fortune to spend time with a wildly eclectic group of people – artists, designers, engineers, musicians, filmmakers, and, of course, athletes. We encourage Nike designers and communicators to do the same. This kind of interaction results in some interesting collaborations that pull us out of the comfort zone. The deeper insights gained from making the right connections are invaluable. Besides, it's a lot more fun than P&L analysis.

The deeper insights you gain from making the right connections are invaluable.

Twenty-five years ago when I first came to Nike, I was lucky enough to work with two people who really defined the creative emphasis at Nike, Bill Bowerman and Jeff Johnson. As is often the case with wizards, they were alternately charming and cantankerous, generous and demanding, but both were equally fixated on innovation, deeply devoted to making sure that what we were creating actually helped the athlete perform better.

My job is to help carry that torch, to make sure our passion for real innovation continues to thrive.

Create an Innovative Environment

❶ Create SWAT Teams – Does your company use hothouses or SWAT teams currently? If not, consider assembling a diverse team around a specific innovation issue. The key is to insulate them from the day-to-day demands of the business.

❷ Think about Team Chemistry – Mark has a real talent for understanding how to put together a dynamic team. When constructing your teams, bring together a group of personalities who work well together. They will probably outperform a team with one or two big egos.

❸ Create Organic Teams – When you need to tap into innovation quickly, put together the kind of team that makes sense for the situation. Sometimes it can be one person charged with figuring out a problem by getting out into the marketplace and exploring options. Other times it takes a highly skilled team. Constantly experiment with the kind of teams you assemble to innovate.

❹ Find the Balance between Structure and Creativity – To stay innovative, it is critical to constantly seek out balance between structure and chaos, especially for the teams trying to innovate. Change things up if necessary to keep people focused on the main goal of co-creating innovation.

❺ Focus on Open Communication – One of the stumbling blocks to which many innovative teams fall victim is a feeling of disconnectedness from the rest of the company. Many times, it feels as if nobody really cares.

Likewise, others in the company might feel the special group is full of dreamers doing nothing to achieve the goals of the company. The key is to appoint a co-creation evangelist on the team whose job is communicating with the rest of the organization about what the team is doing. Invite others to participate in the team's co-creation.

❻ Support Varied Innovation – Innovation is a messy business. Mark's experience at Nike proves it is critical to try lots of different avenues to birth successful innovation. Look at an innovation problem from many different angles. Support different efforts in pursuing co-creation with different stakeholders. One team might pursue co-creating new innovation with a supplier while another team gains the customer perspective.

❼ Identify Generalists – Often the strongest person in the innovation process is a generalist inside the company. Early in Mark's career, one of his bosses recognized that he was a generalist who knew a lot about many different aspects of making shoes. Mark's broad knowledge gave him a unique ability not only to work with others but also to see connections that others might not. Identify generalists that can benefit the innovation team. They will bring a new perspective to the co-creative process.

_____

_____

_____

_____

_____

_____

_____

_____

_____

_____

_____

_____

_____

_____

_____

Create an Innovative Environment

Think about ways to bring more flexibility into your innovation practice. Can you pull diverse teams together to solve problems that need quick answers? Think about making this team more diverse by bringing in an unusual mix of talent. Draw a diagram of this new team and the problem it needs to solve

Create an Innovative Environment

1. Nike's Web site: http://www.nike.com.

2. *When Teams Work Best: 6,000 Team Members and Leaders Tell What it Takes to Succeed* by F. LaFasto and C. Larson (Sage). The authors interviewed over 6,000 team members and leaders about working relationships and collaboration.

3. "In Search of Reflective Behavior and Shared Understanding in Ad Hoc Expert Teams" by I. Mulder, J. Swaak, and J. Kessels, *CyberPsychology & Behavior* 7, no. 2 (April 2004): 141. The authors focus on virtual ad hoc expert teams for the integration of learning and working, as ad hoc teams seem to be one way to cope with complexity in a knowledge-intensive society.

4. "The Teamster" by Jennifer Vilaga, *Fast Company*, April 2005, 94. This is a good primer on the Managing Teams for Innovation and Success course offered at Stanford University.

5. "When Meeting Targets Becomes the Strategy, CEO Is on Wrong Path" by Carol Hymowitz, *Wall Street Journal*, March 8, 2005,. B1. Hymowitz suggests that if meeting sales and profit targets is all that is expected from a manager, the company will suffer.

6. "Want Collaboration?" by Jeff Weiss and Jonathan Hughes, *Harvard Business Review* 83, no. 3 (March 2005): 93. The authors point out that team leaders get truly effective collaboration only when they realize that conflict is natural and necessary.

7. "Nurturing Creativity" by Dan German, *Brand Strategy*, February 2005,15. German focuses on the effort to maintain creativity in a growing business.

8. "The Gift of ADHD" by Anne Underwood, *Newsweek*, March 14, 2005, 48. Underwood talks about the controversial notion that distractibility, poor impulse control, and emotional sensitivity have other sides that are actually strengths, such as creativity, energy, and intuition.

9. *Breakthrough: Stories and Strategies of Radical Innovation* by Mark Stefik and Barbara Stefik (MIT Press). The Stefiks look at the trend toward open innovation: acquiring technologies from outside, marketing their technologies to other companies, and outsourcing manufacturing.

10. *Seeing What's Next: Using Theories of Innovation to Predict Industry Change* by Clayton M. Christensen, Erik A. Roth, and Scott D. Anthony (Harvard Business School Press). It's always good to keep up with Clayton's writing. The authors offer a framework for predicting industry winners and losers.

11. "Poetry in the Boardroom: Thinking Beyond the Facts," *Journal of Business Strategy* 26, no. 1 (2005): 34. This is a good look at the relationship between reading poetry and strategic thinking.

12. "Managers and Leaders: Are They Different?" by Abraham Zaleznik, *Harvard Business Review* 82, no. 1 (January 2004): 74. This is a classic article, reprinted from 1977, that discusses proposed differences between managers and leaders.

13. "What It Takes to Innovate" by Paola Hjelt, *Fortune*, March 7, 2005, 52. This article focuses on the idea that companies need more than good ideas to be great innovators. They also need a vision, a plan, and the right people in the right places.

14. "The 6 Myths of Creativity" by Bill Breen, *Fast Company*, December 2004, 75. Breen does a wonderful job of clarifying issues around corporate creativity.

15. "The Fabric of Creativity" by Alan Deutschman, *Fast Company*, December 2004, 54. This is a great article on W.L. Gore & Associates and its knack for innovation built from a culture where people feel free to pursue ideas on their own, communicate with one another, and collaborate out of self-motivation rather than a sense of duty.

When Henry Beer enters a room, his energy is overwhelming. Henry is as comfortable talking about the winner of a stage in the Tour de France, a local zoning issue, global politics, or the effects of design on innovation. Whenever I am stuck on a creative problem, Henry is at the top of my list of people to call for help in getting energized or to look at a problem with renewed vigor and excitement. In fact, following most of our conversations, my head is spinning from the introduction of so many new ideas and possibilities.

After working for the office of Charles Eames, Henry co-founded Communication Arts in Boulder, Colorado, in 1973. Henry's work has helped redefine the way people interact with space, especially retail and public space, with projects in such places as New York, Tokyo, Singapore, Barcelona, and downtown Boulder. In fact, one of the first projects his firm did, recreating Pearl Street from one of the busiest streets in downtown Boulder to a pedestrian mall, helped usher in an era of urban renewal.

I wanted to tap into Henry's mind to consider ways to organize space for the purpose of co-creating innovation. His ideas about workspace as a creative tool, using visual triggers, the cross-pollination of ideas, creating space for accidental intersections, and creating your own lens are foundational in being co-creative with an innovation team. Henry's perspective takes the paradigm of most companies — to establish a space and expect the individuals and the type of work to mold to that space — and reverses it. He suggests that the space itself is a creative tool and must be as flexible and able to change and adapt as the people who work within it.

Inspiration

There are design firms where you walk into the office and everything is completely and totally organized, and there is absolutely no question you're in a real design environment. We are much less rigorous than that, and we are far more likely to be focused on our projects and our interactions than we are on the specifics of the envelope. For us, a great work environment is the absence of things rather than the presence of things – it is the absence of a program so relentless that you feel you've got to shape yourself to accommodate the space instead of having the space be flexible.

Your Office as an Instrument

My favorite story about workplaces is the old media lab at MIT, an old ramshackle wooden building that was beloved by every scientist and by every technologist and engineer who ever worked there. The thing was like a great big tool. If you were doing an experiment, you could nail directly to the floors, you could rivet whatever you wanted to the walls, you could cut holes to run pipes, because the building itself was seen as an integral instrument of creativity.

When we moved into our office, we just created space; we created volume. We were not obsessed with making an architectural or design statement with the building – for us the building is the picture frame, not the picture. The picture is the work, the people, the interaction, and the energy our clients invariably recognize when they come into the building.

Ebbs and Flows

I think that, if anything, the ebbing and flowing of work and the ebbing and flowing of numbers of employees, the expansion and contraction, all make it very difficult to plan for having a great deal of collaborative space. Sometimes, collaborative space is open when the work is slow and there's not much to collaborate on, but when it's busy, all the collaborative space is filled with people doing work. So it's the volatility of the creative business once again, being able to plan and order and organize in a way that a business has less volatility. This business is perpetually entrepreneurial, because we constantly have to invent and generate ideas, and we are subject to the most volatile component of all of the market sectors we work – the development sector. Sometimes it's good; sometimes it's not so good.

> For us the building is the picture frame, not the picture.

Create Visual Triggers

Obviously there's a very limited amount of linearity around here. If you want a linear mind, you have to go somewhere else. The linear mind tends to want a physical environment that is more rigorous, where everything is sort of on the X/Y axis and carefully aligned. We're all about just making sure there are a lot of visual triggers around. I think it's no accident that we pin things on the wall, because we want to be perpetually invigorated by these ideas and images. Every surface in this office is a visual resource for creativity – not because it was designed to be, but that's just the way we use space.

Own the Design

> Every surface in this office is a visual resource for creativity.

We recently went through the process of redesigning the office of a preeminent law firm that moved into a new space, and we had lots of ideas about what that space should be. The process of allowing people in that practice to contribute to a description and the creation of the characteristics or principles that the office should exhibit gave them a sense of propriety and ownership. Short of actually having them design their own space, our hope was that when they walked into the office, the design brief would be pinned up in the lobby and they'd go down the list and say, "You know what, we did all of this; we had a voice in this."

Personalize Your Space

There are some corporate cultures like this one that encourage people to make the space their own. Then there are other corporate cultures where the idea is to subvert the identity of people so they participate in a larger identity. There are complaints about those kinds of workspaces – they are felt to be sterile or hermetic or constraining. But every workspace doesn't have to look like a day care center either. That ability to personalize a space, to have things that are an expression of your life beyond the confines of the work environment, is crucial to promoting a sense of open-mindedness. I don't care whether you're running a law practice or a design firm or whatever it is – creativity can inhabit any profession.

> Creativity, in essence, is making connections between things that are out there.

Make the Connections

Creativity, in essence, is making connections between things that are out there; everybody looks at the same thing, but no two people make the same connection. It's that openness, it's looking, it's the punch line of a joke – that's the ultimate expression of creativity. It takes you somewhere you never expected to go, even though you thought you knew where you were going. So around here, those little visual trigger mechanisms are intellectual to some people; to others they are mathematical or scientific. I think that whatever language you operate in on a day-to-day basis, there needs to be a physical expression of that language somewhere that's available to your other senses – I think that's a fundamental requirement in any creative workspace.

It's important to express these values both implicitly and explicitly – as benefits to employees, existing and potential clients, or colleagues and professionals from affiliated consultancies who might be interested in becoming a part of the practice. Recruiting is a huge thing – the work environment can have a material effect on how people view themselves. If a person walked into the office and thought, "This is me," that's great. But what if that person walks in and says, "This is who I could be"? That's even better, because it's inspirational.

In any industry, the quality of recruiting is important. For example, a young engineering student might walk into the old MIT Media Lab and say, "This is Toyland; this is how I work, this is how my garage lab was," as opposed to that same kid walking into the new I.M. Pei–designed building reacting, "What the hell is this? I can't work this way." Branding, or making sure the environment reflects the values and virtues of the organization for better or for worse, is

> What we try to do, or what we have accomplished, is to create a space where accidental couplings or pairings can happen.

crucial. Otherwise, you're sending either a disingenuous message or, at worst, a dishonest message about who you really are.

Encourage Cross-Pollination

In our business, cross-pollination is everything – ideas propagate other ideas. What we try to do, or what we have accomplished, is to create a space where accidental couplings or pairings can happen as somebody's walking by someone else's desk. Because the whole workspace is open, we can always look over everybody else's desk. I call this "work reviews." We don't do formal work reviews around here, because work reviews are done every day while we're walking around looking at what people are doing. I can be standing at the printer and can tell what people are doing, without having to sit down and have a formal review. The good news is that it enables people to intersect each other – to share ideas, to not hoard – and that's kind of the ethos around here. This workspace is the physical embodiment of that sensibility.

The workplace is an integral part of the work product.

Create Intersection Space

There's a big engineering company in Germany – very, very typical of all the German clichés you can imagine related to the building and workspace and everything else. But one inspired thing this company did was to cut a giant hole between the floors and put in a staircase that goes from the top of the building all the way to the bottom. It's a very wide staircase, and what they're really hoping will happen as people going up and down the stairs (instead of riding an elevator) is that they'll intersect each other. They'll talk to each other, and even better, they'll sit on the stairs

– like the Spanish steps in Rome. It really becomes a kind of accessed sociability that once again will encourage chance cross-pollination.

Even the more conventional businesses that don't look at the workspace as a tool are beginning to recognize the possibilities. I think there's definitely increased perception that, in fact, the workplace is an integral part of the work product. If you choose to ignore it, you might leave a lot of money on the table, leave a lot of potential and opportunity there, compared to what it could be were you to have a space that was more supportive of what you're trying to do.

It's really interesting to look at old office buildings, where everyone was in small offices with hammered glass partitions so you couldn't see in. The proverbial private-eye's office was actually the model for all workspaces, and the idea of open offices and pools of people was really a response to the stultifying nature of those old work environments.

When we started in this building, a few of us did have offices. And at one point we were on two floors, which was terrible – people felt completely separate and alienated. So we had to add on so all of us could be on the same floor – we just had to.

> It really becomes a kind of accessed sociability that once again will encourage that chance cross-pollination.

Focus Your Own Lens

To *innovate* – if you look at the roots of the word – is to look at something familiar anew. It's to reinvigorate the way you see things, like a computer screen that's constantly refreshing itself. Innovation is something that can be learned, but it can't be taught – like a bunch of ornithologists sitting around wishing they were birds; they're never going to fly. They might know everything there is to know about the subject, but they're still not birds. I think innovation is a way of looking at the world irrespective of your background, whether you're a scientist, an engineer, an artist, an accountant, a lawyer, or whatever it is – a person who is just not satisfied using a lens that was ground by someone else. You have to grind your own lens, and to me a good workplace is a lab that allows you to grind your own lens, so that the focus and the perspective and the fall-off is just what you want, as opposed to what somebody else says you want.

Innovation is something that can be learned, but it can't be taught.

Space Matters

❶ Make Space Flexible – Innovation is not a linear process, and the workspace for it needs to reflect this. Space for an innovation team needs to be flexible so that different people can come together in different situations to create. Be sure that the space accommodates you instead of you accommodating the space.

❷ Make Space an Instrument of Creativity – Make your innovation space an integral part of the creative activity of innovation. In fact, let the team design it themselves. Creativity can be a volatile process. Try to minimize the volatility level by keeping the costs down and the space simple. Focus on the function of the space rather than the form.

❸ Construct Visual Triggers – Use surfaces of the office to inspire innovation and allow for lots of room for inspiration. One company I've worked with even has small offices that act as project-specific war rooms, where all of the visual inspiration of a specific project is allowed to exist. People on the team can use the room for working or conducting meetings, all the while being inspired by the visual cues in the room.

❹ Innovation is Messy; Allow for It – Many companies have rigid rules for office design: the same size cubicle for everyone, allowing only certain personal items to be displayed. It seems that the accountants in the office have designed the space to be efficient. But innovation needs space to try things. It requires the spirit of a workshop.

❺ Encourage Cross-Pollination – Innovation is all about making new connections, seeing things in a different light and expanding on the insight. To make this happen, encourage the cross-pollination of ideas by creating an open environment where people walk around and comment on each other's work in progress. Instead of having review meetings of the innovation work, support an environment of constant co-creation.

❻ Create Intersection Spaces – The best innovation often happens in the hallways and at the water cooler. Create space for people to hang out and chat. It could be a cubicle with an old couch and some chairs. Throw in a coffee maker and allow people to meet, relax, and co-create. By creating this intersection space, mental space is also created and allows more creative thinking.

❼ Innovation Is Personal – Even if you're on a team, the act of innovating is a very personal and human one. Encourage people to, as Henry says, "grind their own lens." The development of one's lens is a direct result of experience. Encourage the participation of everyone; require individuals to have a point of view, backed up with evidence of their own experience.

Interaction

_____

_____

_____

_____

_____

_____

_____

_____

_____

_____

_____

_____

_____

Space Matters

Think about your company's space. Consider ways to promote flow, create intersection spaces, and cut down on formal reviews and meetings by changing the way your office is laid out. In the process, be more innovative. Draw a new office layout for your company. What does it look like right now? What might it look like?

Resources

1. **Communication Arts' Web site**: http://www.commarts-boulder.com.

2. **"Brainsketching and How it Differs from Brainstorming"** by Remko van der Lugt, *Creativity & Innovation Management* 11, no. 1 (March 2002): 43. Brainsketching is an interesting idea-generation technique based on brainwriting that uses sketching as the primary means of recording ideas.

3. **"Creativity in Communication: A Theoretical Framework for Collaborative Product Creation"** by Stephan Sonnenburg, *Creativity & Innovation Management* 13, no. 4 (December 2004): 254. Sonnenburg looks at creativity in the context of collaboration.

4. **"Strategic Intensity"** by Diane L. Coutu, *Harvard Business Review* 83, no. 4 (April 2005): 49. In an interview with world chess champion Garry Kasparov, Coutu looks at the importance of intensity in solving a problem.

5. *Chaos, Management and Economics: The Implications of Non-linear Thinking* by David Parker and Ralph Stacey (London: Institute of Economic Affairs). The authors examine the concept of chaos theory and how it can be applied to the social sciences.

6. **"Time, Knowledge and Evolutionary Dynamics: Why Connections Matter"** by Brian J. Loasby, *Journal of Evolutionary Economics* 11, no. 4:393. The author looks at how human cognition relies less on logic than on pattern making.

7. *Creating Workplaces Where People Can Think* by Phyl Smith and Lynn Kearny (Jossey-Bass). Smith and Kearny explore how design problems in an organization may interfere with performance.

8. *Creating the Project Office: A Manager's Guide to Leading Organizational Change* by Randall L. Englund, Robert J. Graham, and Paul C. Dinsmore (Jossey-Bass). This book is a good guide to help those searching for ways to transform their organizations into more effective and efficient project-based workplaces.

9. *The Designer's Workspace: Ultimate Office Design* by Douglas B. Caywood (Architectural Press). A good resource on how firms respond to the challenge of designing their own offices.

10. GreatBuildings.com: http://www.greatbuildings.com/. This is a good architecture Web site.

11. The Architecture and Design Collection, Museum of Modern Art in New York: http://www.moma.org/collection/depts/arch_design/. This Web site is another great one for inspiration.

12. Archpedia.com: http://www.archpedia.com. An independent Web site with information about architecture and architectural styles, articles, and a dictionary of architectural terms.

Very early in the creation of Spark, I had a conversation that astonished me with Scott Bowers, Oakley's vice president of marketing worldwide. It was Oakley's idea to always ask themselves if their decisions were brave enough. This inspired me to think about innovation in a different way. The idea of bravery is certainly at the core of co-creating innovation, but it is hard to be brave constantly. I know from firsthand experience that when I'm running a successful company, sooner or later I start making safer decisions than when I was a start-up and willing to risk everything on a passionate idea.

Oakley has done a great job of continually innovating outside the comfort zone. As an observer, I am always amazed how Oakley takes an idea for a new product like a watch, pushes the limits of design – Oakley's first watch cost $1,500 – and then takes those learnings and creates modified versions of the designs that, in context, don't seem so out there. Instead of following a linear, evolutionary path for innovation, Oakley takes a braver, more revolutionary strategy. They'll see how far they can push an innovation, get the buzz from the effort, and then make the innovation more accessible. This revolutionary model requires bravery, and Oakley thrives on it.

All of us could act with more bravery in the way we think about innovation. Scott lays the foundation for being brave by discussing being open, more spontaneous, and more human, by fighting mediocrity and safety in a way that inspires us all to be more brave in co-creating innovations, in all aspects of our lives.

Scott Bowers — Be Brave

I've had the blessing of working for Oakley for 18 years, and I was an athlete for Oakley for about 5 years prior to that. I've played different roles here, everything from a sports marketing manager to a sales manager to vice president of sports marketing to my current role as vice president of marketing worldwide.

Go with Your Gut

I have had the benefit of working with both a CEO and president who in a sense are "look and feel directors" and who instill a real sense of bravery when it comes to the direction of the brand. A lot of our business is about just understanding where the brand is. What we need to change comes from the gut instincts of employees within or from having a dialogue with certain partners we have internally – athletes, media partners, or retail partners.

Besides the instinctual senses of our founder and president, this is how we really get a sense of where the brand is positioned. We have never relied on traditional research, believing that most of it is homogenized to meet the needs of those acquiring it for us, who basically tell us either what we want to hear or what we don't want to hear. It's never really done in a format where we can trust whoever's doing the research for us. We are also skeptical of what consumers – typical consumers – want. Not to sound brandcentric, but each time we've given the market what it wants, we end up just following what everybody else is doing. Instead, we strive to be brave and design or develop products that really build on what already exists and just make it better. We let the design and the technology drive our brand instead of trying to follow what the trends might be or what research might tell us.

Solve Problems

Leaders don't follow. It might make for ups and downs in business, but in the end a brave brand sustains trends. However, you can't be different just to be different; you have to have purpose and substance. Your products and marketing must be relevant and make a difference to your core consumers' lives. Our founder's mantra is to "solve problems with invention and wrap those inventions in art." To me this statement breaks us away from those brands that merely follow trends, slap a logo on their product,

> We strive to be brave and design or develop products that really build on what already exists.

and throw out a fancy and overpaid marketing campaign. Consumers ultimately gravitate to products that are unique and meaningful. Sure, they may chase brands that are hot for an instant, but for 100-year brands it's not about the battle but the war. Be brave and authentic, and sustain the ups and downs that trends may bring.

At Oakley, "bravery" is spoken often, and it comes in many forms, especially product design and technology. We frequently say, "Let's do something that is daring and breakaway and challenges conventional thinking." It's also a matter of zigging when everyone else is zagging – be the shepherd, not the sheep. In marketing, we identify with athletes or key influencers who might not win every event but are the most rebellious and most outspoken. Ultimately, they are the most colorful, media visible, and marketable. "Let's just do things that go against the grain of mediocrity." This message really comes from all of us in senior management, especially Jim Jannard, our founder, and Colin Baden, our president. They constantly push us out of our comfort zone. Sometimes, there is a push back, but we always end up in a braver position.

> Be brave and authentic, and sustain the ups and downs that trends may bring.

Be Champions of Your Brand

It is crucial within the organization that senior management and the various groups we manage all support this same attitude. We typically look at the design, marketing – especially alternative sports marketing – and sales teams as being the ultimate "champions" of the brand, the real opinion leaders among all the employees. To move the majority of the employee population, it is crucial that the calculated risk-taking attitude that comes from the self-appointed champions of the organization trickle down to all the various departments. Bravery is an action. If the champions of the organization express bravery and confidence, others will follow and soon champion the brand as well. But there has to be complete belief and support in the direction the brand wants to go and in the products that are subsequently designed. The direction must first be succinctly described and communicated. If it's not, the majority of employees may not see it and understand it, and the brand can easily slip back to its comfort zone.

Be Visible

At Oakley, we have a typical organizational structure on paper, but that's about as far as it goes. To us, titles restrict thinking and growth, especially when they control the layers below from communicating up. We really try to induce the entire company to have a very open-minded, open-dialogue attitude. This comes all the way down from our top management. We dislike closed-door offices – we prefer to be visible and approachable. It instigates spontaneous, rich communication and breaks down the closed-door,

> We really try to induce the entire company to have a very open-minded, open-dialogue attitude.

you-will-hear-what-senior-management-wants-you-to-hear attitude. I want my employees to hear my dialogue. I want them to build a common way of communicating the message of the brand. Feel it, live it, communicate it.

Communicate Face-to-Face

We're also starting to find that while e-mail and, specifically, Blackberries were great communication tools in the beginning, they tend to close off real communication because people just fire off e-mails all day long. They manage by desktop. We are devising different ways of communicating that get people back together and communicating face-to-face. We try to promote smaller discussions that get a group focused on something, and from there the group can go out and convey the message to others within the organization.

> We are devising different ways of communicating that get people back together and communicating face-to-face.

Take Time to Get Out

The marketing group has to maintain open-minded creativity all the time. However, it is still easy to get caught up in the minutiae and forget why we're here – to be creative and to figure out unique ways to portray the brand. I can recognize that in my key employees, so sometimes I force them to get out of the office to do something, especially the favored activities of our core customers. Uniquely, our employees work at Oakley because it portrays their individual lifestyle. Most of our employees participate in the sports that Oakley lives and breathes every day. This is a critical formula in connecting to and being authentic to our target market.

When you're able to create a corporate lifestyle that is similar to the day-to-day lifestyle of your

employees to a point where it integrates itself, that's when you're going to get the maximum out of your employees. It may be just being able to come in and speak the language of their recreation and their business, but at the same time you still need to be sensitive and make sure they get out and participate in those hobbies, or sooner or later they are either going to lose interest in what they're doing or just get burned out. You become what you are. You've constantly got to instill in your employees the idea that they've got to get out and do the things they came to work believing they'd be involved with.

Share Experiences

I think we're all pretty integrated and have the same attitudes and ideas. Not only do we have time to go enjoy what we like to do, but we come back and talk about it. When we talk about those experiences, that in itself can instigate communication on why we need to do things in certain areas, or to help us dream up ideas that might be more effective. I guess that's the benefit of a company that really instills a lifestyle of some sort; it's so important because, one, we're a lot more energetic about the job we do and, two, we're

It's hugely important to have our employees deeply entrenched in the sports in which we really need to keep our finger on the pulse of.

talking and walking and living what we love.

On the marketing side, it's hugely important to have our employees deeply entrenched in the sports in which we really need to keep our finger on the pulse of. Our employees participate in every single sport we're involved with, especially on the sports marketing side. These guys live that life, walk the walk, and talk the talk. And if they see that we're headed in the wrong direction, their bullshit meter goes off in a hurry. They're pushed to do so. If we're doing an ad creative that doesn't align with a particular sports industry, then the guys who know and live those sports are relied on to say, "Hey, this ad sucks. We look like a bunch of poseurs."

> When they live that life day in and day out, they know what's real and what's right for the brand, and are able to connect to the brand.

Live the Lifestyle

We are often asked the question, Do you go out and talk to your customers? When I look at our sports marketing team especially, we talk to our customers every day. But it's more than that; it is living the lives of our customers who participate in those sports or lifestyles. We have a lot of athletes and ex-athletes who are now designers. We have a sports marketing team made up of 25 employees, and the majority

of them are ex-professional athletes. Now they go back in and market their sport, and the reason we've preferred to hire ex-athletes versus somebody with a degree is that they really know how to live the life of that sport. They know every little intricacy that it takes to bring complete authenticity and legitimacy to the brand, and we tap into them every single day. Fortunately, we have a design team that's very similar – a lot of the guys are into motocross and surf, mountain bike, skate, or snowboard – and when they live that life day in and day out, they know what's real and what's right for the brand, and are able to connect to the brand.

This is where being brave comes in. You know, Oakley went through a pretty big transition recently, and we're far from through with it, but fortunately I think we're over the first hurdle. Any brand, especially a niche brand that gains popularity or success, runs the biggest risk of becoming too mainstream and not being considered cool anymore. I've seen Oakley go through probably five different cycles – and the brands that can succeed are the ones that recognize when they've gone mainstream or that their age demographic has gotten older and then can turn the company on a dime to reconnect with the core audience that they know can really drive trends for the future.

> It is scary to take risks, but play it too safe, and you will find yourself in a much worse situation down the road.

Take Risks, Make Decisions

The brands that are brave enough to say, "You know what – we're selling way too much of the wrong product to the wrong people," will always remain progressive. The brands that are willing to change the language of the brand and the face of the brand and be brave with product design can turn themselves around and sustain greater longevity as a brand. It is scary to take risks, but play it too safe while chasing numbers and quarterly reports, and you will find yourself in a much worse situation down the road.

It's very easy to be a cool brand; it's a piece of cake to make a brand cool. The tough part for those cool brands once they become successful is to stay cool or become cool again. You've got to have a management team that can recognize that quickly, be brave enough to take chances, and not rely on tons of information to confirm what they see. Last, be fluid enough to get employees to embrace it and turn it around.

> Decisions need to come from the gut, and they need to come from those who deeply understand what the brand was built on.

Stay Brave

The biggest piece of advice I can offer, what I would really push to others, is to remain brave, don't stray from your core essence or beliefs, and don't get caught up in the minutiae that distract you from instinctual decision making. Decisions need to come from the gut, and they need to come from those who deeply understand what the brand was built on. I see this fault in a lot of larger brands that have lost the "gatekeepers" who instinctually know and understand what the brand ultimately stands for. You need instinctual leaders who can make quick, brave decisions. If the decision is miscalculated, it can always be changed later, but as long as a decision is being made and action taken on it, things will always move forward, especially if you've built an infrastructure of employees around you who "get it."

I've watched so many companies get so caught up in the personal agenda, minutiae, and process that it just immobilizes them. It literally stops them dead in their tracks. What was once a brave and innovative idea becomes so watered down it becomes safe and ineffective. We have a saying at Oakley – "Adapt, improvise, and overcome." If you do make a wrong decision, you see what was wrong about it and adjust and build on it.

The senior management ultimately determines how brave a brand can be. A lack of bravery stifles progress. If the senior management is brave but also smart and calculating, then the rest of the company will follow suit. If you have a conservative upper management that's not willing to take calculated risks, well, that hesitancy is just going to trickle down to everyone.

A lack of bravery stifles progress.

Tools

Be Brave

❶ Trust Your Intuition – It's so easy to want to analyze more information when trying to make a business decision. Yet going with your gut gives you the ability to innovate more quickly and creatively in today's uncertain environment. To practice, try making smaller decisions more spontaneously. Make the decision that "feels" right without having all the data.

❷ Connect with Key Voices – Oakley knows the key voices for its business. It is the minds of unconventional thinkers, professional athletes, and specialty retailers that are the opinion leaders in the marketplace. Who are the key voices in your marketplace? Get out and spend time with them. Invite them to co-create innovation with you.

❸ Go Against the Grain of Mediocrity – Don't get stuck being mediocre. While being in a safe place and wanting things to be predictable might work well in some areas of business, it won't work when it comes to innovation. If there is a process that feels safe yet inhibiting, it's probably fueling mediocrity. Think about ways to break out of it.

❹ Identify Risk-Takers – Think about people who take risks in your company. Seek them out. Meet with them. Invite them to lunch. Better yet, get them in a position to help co-create innovation. Absorb some of their positive energy. Risk-takers can be found at every level and in every facet of an organization.

❺ Use Less Technology – Communication technologies like e-mail are wonderfully efficient tools but are a poor substitute for spending time with the people inside and outside your company. If you really want to make things happen, you've got to make eye contact with your partners in co-creation and innovation. Virtual technologies should only support such human encounters.

❻ Know Your Corporate Lifestyle – How closely aligned is your corporate lifestyle with the lifestyle of your employees? Companies that understand their employees well and can provide an environment that supports their lifestyles have a better chance of attracting and keeping the best and most creative people.

❼ Continue to Take Risks – Most companies, at their core, are based on innovation. The company's founder likely took an entrepreneurial risk and made something happen. Yet as successful companies mature, they naturally take fewer risks and try to preserve what they have. The world is too disruptive today for a company to survive in such a defensive posture. By taking risks, innovation is given the fertile environment it needs to thrive.

Interaction

_____

_____

_____

_____

_____

_____

_____

_____

_____

_____

_____

_____

_____

_____

_____

Be Brave

Think about your company and how it approaches innovation. Are you brave enough? Do you really think about and strive for innovation unshackled from your company's constraints – both real and perceived? Describe three things you can (and should) do to make your company braver.

Resources

1. Web site: http://www.oakley.com.

2. "Going Above and Beyond: The Emotional Labor of Adventure Guides" by Erin K. Sharpe, *Journal of Leisure Research* 37, no. 1 (2005): 29. This author provides an account of the emotional labor of adventure guides at Wanderlust, an outdoor adventure trip provider.

3. "Just Risk It" by Hank Kim and T. L. Stanley, *Advertising Age*, February 9, 2004. This article explores the significance of taking risks and experimentation with alternative advertising platforms for brand marketers.

4. "Bold Type: How Risk Takers Can Change the Media Industry" by Nick Brien, *Adweek*, February 11, 2002. Brien offers five tactics for making boldness work in branding strategy.

5. "Sex Doesn't Sell," *Economist*, October 30, 2004, 62. The article explores how, according to advertisers, sex no longer sells the way it used to in Great Britain.

6. "The Collaborator" by Victoria Murphy, *Forbes*, March 14, 2005, 73. This article profiles technosocial scientist Brian Behlendorf, creator of Apache, and his mission to influence the way people regard software.

7. "Working to Live or Living to Work? Work/Life Balance Early in the Career" by Jane Sturges and David Guest, *Human Resource Management Journal* 14, no. 4: 5. This article explores the relationships between work/life balance, work/nonwork conflict, hours worked, and company commitment.

8. Joy at Work: A Revolutionary Approach to Fun on the Job by Dennis W. Bakke (PVG). The founder of the international energy giant AES talks about worker autonomy and self-determination.

9. "Why We all Need to Get Out More" by David Nicholson-Lord, *New Statesman*, January 24, 2005, 32. Nicholson-Lord argues that being indoors has negative results for people's social and cultural lives, as well as for their health.

10. "Brave New Wardrobe" by Dan Tynan, *PC World*, April 2005, 118. This article covers information about wearable computing, including the Oakley Thump Sunglasses and MP3 player.

11. "Taking Risks with Advertising: The Case of the Not-for-Profit Sector" by Douglas West and Adrian Sargeant, *Journal of Marketing Management* 20, no. 9/10 (November 2004): 1027. This article examines the advertising risk-taking propensity of not-for-profit organizations.

Marsha is one of those very cool people who just exemplify the image of an innovative designer. She's calm, thoughtful, and inspiring, always bringing out the best in everyone in a conversation. Speaking with Marsha always leaves me feeling like I've had a wonderful meal; it's so satisfying.

Marsha has been at Herman Miller for 27 years and has played eight major roles in her time there. Hence, I thought it would be great to talk with her about how an innovative company like Herman Miller keeps coming up with such great furniture innovations. I think Marsha's interview is an especially nice complement to Mark Parker's perspective. While Mark has an amazing vision about co-creating innovation and the ability to support teams to get work done at Nike, Marsha has been in the trenches, participating on many such teams being innovative at Herman Miller.

Marsha's ideas about making innovation iterative, creating the right conditions for innovation, and focusing on keeping the momentum going are important concepts for any company striving to be more innovative.

Inspiration

I'm currently leading a market response effort with a design and development (D&D) unit that will take the product needs and pending customer projects, do development around project activity, and maintain the products in the current customer-need realm. Meanwhile, another core D&D group will work on the future leaps out five to ten years from now. So I'm doing the problem definition and the work around what people need today and how fast we can get it to them. Part of the need for this role, which hasn't existed before, comes from the belief that we need to have some work that speculates on the future and that there's a way to innovate by really understanding current problems in depth, in real time, and solving to those. This can evolve a product almost on a day-to-day basis and lead to innovative thinking.

Collaborate

Certain products innovate from an extreme intimacy with a problem by getting tightly connected with user issues. In one case, the problem involved issues around comfort and sitting, so the final product evolved from the designer's views about the heat that's generated from the body in contact with the chair. If there's discomfort inherent in sitting in a chair, how do we alleviate that problem? So the initial answer was an aerated seat, which led to how we accomplish that. And so the designers kept diving deeper into that problem and took the same approach on all elements of the design. It was a collaboration between the designer and the engineers, both looking deeply into the issues and working to deconstruct and rebuild them with a different view.

Think About Customer Behavior

I think we have a good history of studying user behavior rather than just taking user feedback verbatim; we'll look at it in a deeper way. For example, a team may use imagery, studies, and science around the issues of sitting that users probably aren't even aware of. If we'd done focus groups and asked people what they wanted in a chair, these issues wouldn't come up. Basically, we study users and talk with users about comfort and then interpret those findings into some base problems. I think it's this process that leads us to rethink the whole problem.

> A team will have imagery, studies, and science around the issues of sitting that users probably aren't even aware of.

Deconstruct the Problem

We did the same thing on another design for the building and construction industry on how to power and light space. We innovated by combining gray areas that no one else would tackle. Again, it's deconstructing the problem as a whole and looking at it, not in a clinical way, but as a sort of ideation of where the gaps are and where the integration can occur. We realized that one of the barriers in flexible space was how to distribute power and rearrange lighting quickly and maintain flexibility. Solving this problem involves a lot of trades today, and a lot of highly skilled trades, as well as a lot of complicated planning procedures to the point of almost gutting a space to rewire it.

> It's kind of deconstructing the problem as a whole and looking at it, not in a clinical way, but in a sort of ideation way.

Our team came up with the idea that if you have a very simple operating system in a modular power distribution system, you can reconnect switches and outlets and power distribution electronically or digitally as well as physically. It's a separation of the logical from the physical, so the end result is a system that allows you to point at an appliance and then point at a switch and then you're connected. Today, you would have to rewire the switch and the light, so our solution brings a new flexibility to the space. It's really quite innovative, it's real time, and it's a user interface. Another approach might be to put all the lights on an Internet network and have a very complicated system to control it, but that is really another option for an alternate highly skilled trade to control your space. We took that to a very simplistic level, a kind of point-and-click for real time and user feedback. With the power distribution system, once something is plugged into it, it's automatically on the network.

Then the space elements append from this structure, so you can easily move space divisions or walls and then easily move the lights and technology.

Get the Customer Involved Early

To take that one step further, we employ a discovery process in this development. We didn't take leaps of designing the full thing into design completion. We did a first, functional prototype and then got our first customer to work with us to solve to their need or problem. Then we got a second customer and solved to their problem and iterated the product customer by customer.

Create the Conditions for Innovation

Our overall goal is to design the right conditions for innovation instead of legislating innovation. As an example, during the design process I just talked about, our chief development officer led the need for a different process. Basically, he handpicked a small team – I think we started off with six or seven people – and isolated them from the corporation. The team was outside of the day-to-day business in a separate lab environment to think and focus on the problem. We also hired external designers to work with us. Given that focus and a very aggressive completion date, our

> Our overall goal is to design the right conditions for innovation versus legislating innovation.

mission was to look at a specific problem and have an ideation and physical concept in six months.

Being freed from the day-to-day and other issues, and being able to focus on this problem with a tightly constrained deadline, we were able to create a groundswell to the six-month deadline. With a motivation and a release of energy we just moved toward it. All the chief development officer had to do was keep the momentum going. I think there is some aspect of being released from the current corporate constraints for ideation that is important here.

In a previous process, where we were working toward the final design coming out, something similar occurred. We're very proud of our chair engineering capability, and the group working on that design stayed very focused and motivated on solving the problem, without regard to what else was being done that day or whatever current business was being done.

> If you learn and innovate on an incremental level, a spark can ignite something bigger over the cumulative time of doing smaller improvements.

Incremental Innovation

What I'm doing now is based on the idea that if you learn and innovate on an incremental level, a spark can ignite something bigger over the cumulative time of doing smaller improvements. For instance, if you're focused around this incremental process, you can say, "Okay, with these improvements, if we do a large change to the product, how do we innovate to take in all that we've learned?"

Plant the Seed

At times it can seem that any given innovation team or new thought can create something of an antibody in the company, and we're not immune from that happening. In the example I gave before, there was some resentment toward the team that isolated itself; I think that's a natural human reaction. We weren't necessarily dependent on infusing that idea into the corporation, but saying it could be a business in its own right and so had an autonomy and independence meant we believed it should continue for a while until it was proven. So there was sort of a separation from "Here's a great idea" and "Let's shove it through the corporation." It was more "Let's take this seed and plant it outside and see if we can grow a business that, once proven, will then automatically influence the market and thus our day-to-day business."

The Difficulty of Change

Just imagine if somebody has a really great idea – but it's a big one – and wants to change the company overnight. The muscle and the influence needed to do that almost takes superhuman skills. But what if there are departments and units that innovate on their own project activities and are able to implement that innovation through their own means, without necessarily being dependent on the whole corporation. With a lot of those situations, suddenly the corporation gets more wind in its sails. That's not saying a small unit won't have a big idea, but as far as ownership and taking it further, it doesn't have to be dependent on engaging everyone in the corporation. Even on a project team, especially where you have really good engineers and a design team together, the team will figure out ways to give that innovation a proof of concept, prove its market, and almost get close to implementation before the whole corporation needs to get involved. The point here is that there's an em-

There's an empowerment in taking it as far as you can.

powerment in taking it as far as you can.

I think that people who are worried about the day-to-day can be very distracted by these big ideas, because they anticipate disruption and can be irritated by it. It's great to allow some breathing space there and let people float from one project to the other. Having worked with a team that was very independent, I can come back in the corporation not feeling any dependency on the lockstep that tends to happen. That's very important to me, because then I don't really see the boundaries I might have prior to my experience. I see resources that, if they're not busy, I'll ask to help utilize, and it's not like asking permission or giving an assignment.

> I think that people who are worried about the day-to-day can be very distracted by these big ideas.

Contribution

I've noticed, too, that the really good people I see working and doing innovative things often use the word *contribution*, which is just a new revelation in my mind. Someone who's motivated will say, "I want to work on this; I want to make a contribution." I think that person wants to be a part of it and sees a place where he or she can dive into a problem and produce results, knowing that it's not a lifetime commitment and may not even be a reassignment. It's a way of getting connected.

It's not so much about legislating an idea to go through an organization. There's an attitude and an approach that gets learned. When those people work with others, there's an infusion, even if they create a pace. Someone who comes in who has a little faster pace can rev the motor a little bit. If you're working in a small team that has a tight goal but you have made some breakthroughs, you do have a different pace.

You don't feel that interdependence of, "Well, when the team makes up its mind, I'll make my move." It's more, "We're in this together, so let's go; we'll ask forgiveness later." When in doubt, just make your move, as long as it's not hurting anybody; if somebody blocks it, it's easier to say you're sorry. Sometimes, if you ask for permission, you never make any progress.

Inside/Outside Balance

I have a design degree; I've been with the company in various capacities for 27 years. I've probably had eight different major roles, from customer/technical specifications to project management to product design management to research, in all of which I have had different capacities. I've gone from the top, far end of new business development into the belly of the beast, so to speak, but hopefully what I've learned along the way will serve me well in any new role. The only thing I haven't done is operations, which involves actually making the products. It really speaks a lot for this company, that if someone's eager to do different things, they can pave the road. If you're a person who says, "Give me that problem; I'll solve it," this company will make it happen. I try to tell people here that it's not about one-upmanship or positioning yourself; it's about taking on responsibility and solving problems. That's the road; that's the path to moving around this company and getting the good jobs.

It's not about one-upmanship or positioning yourself; it's about taking on responsibility and solving problems.

❶ Focus on Behavior versus Feedback – Are you listening to your customers and really watching their behavior? I never would have told a designer I needed a mesh chair to keep cool. However, I love sitting in my incredibly comfortable Aeron chair. Your customers can give you a deeply personal understanding of their needs.

❷ Make Innovation Iterative – Instead of trying to solve a big, hairy problem all at once, think about making innovation more iterative. Get prototypes ready and then co-create with customers to dial in the details.

❸ Design Optimal Conditions for Innovation – Being innovative means thinking about the right conditions for innovation. Marsha and her team took on a project that was a big change from office furniture. It meant working with a new kind of customer – general contractors rather than end-users – to more efficiently distribute power. Every customer and culture is different. How can you set the conditions for your team to be more innovative?

❹ Keep the Momentum Going – If you're like me and drink too much coffee, your energy might wane during the day as the caffeine wears off. The same thing happens in an innovation. Find a leader or team member who contributes positive energy and direction to keep the momentum and motivation strong.

❺ Focus on Solving the Problem – Sometimes it's hard to strip away the baggage a company or team brings to an innovation problem. Many times, successful companies have a difficult time staying focused on an innovation problem simply because they're successful. Forget about past success and stay focused on the problem at hand, not just the solution.

❻ Accept Resentment – Being on an innovation team that's separate from the rest of the company and having a more creative mandate means you're working on something new and fun. Eventually, the novelty will wear off, but it's a reality that some people in the company will be jealous of your apparent newfound freedom. They will learn to deal with it, and so should you.

❼ Encourage Contribution – Involve other people in your quest for innovation by asking them to contribute. There may be someone in another department who shares a passion for your project and could contribute positively to your team. Develop a spirit of contribution so that everyone in the company feels vested in the evolution of innovation.

Interaction

_____

_____

_____

_____

_____

_____

_____

_____

_____

_____

_____

_____

_____

_____

Maximize Creative Resources

Make a list of other people who could help your innovation team but are often ignored in the process. Is there someone in finance, production, or human resources? Once you've made the list, recruit these people to the team. They will add a lot to the process of being innovative.

Resources

1. **Herman Miller's Web site**: http://www.hermanmiller.com.

2, **"The Contributions of Different Groups of Individuals to Employees' Creativity"** by Nora Madjar, *Advances in Developing Human Resources* 7, no. 2 (May 2005):. 182. The author focuses on how people contribute to employee – and company – creativity.

3. **"Factors Influencing Individual Creativity in the Workplace: An Examination of Quantitative Empirical Research"** by Toby Marshall Egan, *Advances in Developing Human Resources* 7, no. 2 (May 2005): 160. Egan looks closely at various factors that contribute to individual creativity in the workplace.

4. **"How Strategists Really Think"** by Giovanni Gavetti and Jan W. Rivkin, *Harvard Business Review* 83, no. 4 (April 2005): 54. The article discusses reasoning by analogy and how managers can use analogy as a tool for solving problems.

5. **"What is TRIZ? From Conceptual Basics to a Framework for Research"** by Martin G. Moehrle, *Creativity and Innovation Management* 14, no. 1 (March 2005): 3. This paper introduces six aspects of the theory of inventive problem solving (TRIZ).

6. **Triz Journal Web site**: http://www.triz-journal.com. TRIZ research began with the hypothesis that there are universal principles of invention that are the basis for creative innovations that advance technology.

7. "Order and Disorder in Product Innovation Models"
by Miguel Pina e Cunha and Jorge F.S. Gomes, *Creativity and Innovation Management* 12, no. 3 (September 2003): 174. The authors argue that the conceptual development of product innovation models goes hand in hand with paradigmatic changes in the field of organization science.

8. *Herman Miller: The Purpose of Design* by John Berry (Rizzoli). This is a great look at the history of Herman Miller and design.

9. "Designed to Work" by Chuck Slater, *Fast Company*, April 2000, 255. This article looks at Resolve, an office environment created by Herman Miller.

10. Dexigner Design Portal:http://www.dexigner.com/. This site provides the design world with online news.

11. *Weird Ideas That Work: 11 1/2 Practices for Promoting, Managing, and Sustaining Innovation* by Robert I. Sutton (Free Press). This is a fun look at different ideas pertaining to innovation.

12. "Taming Your Tech" by David LaGesse, *U.S. News & World Report*, March 14, 2005, 48. The author discusses elements of user-friendly design in technology.

The Customer

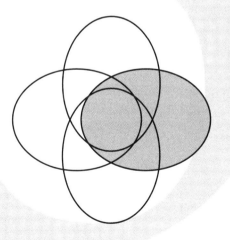

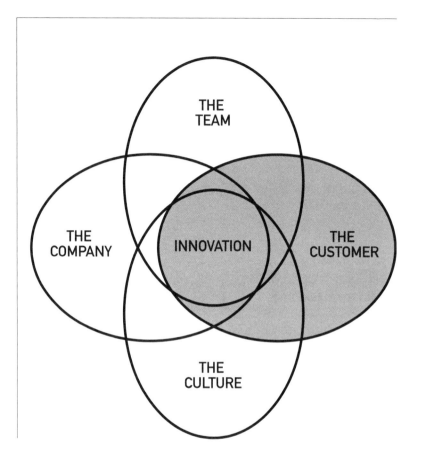

A major driver of innovation is the ability to understand your customers well enough to anticipate what products and services might be needed, by getting out of the office and exploring their world. Many companies focus their innovation efforts around current market needs by relying on traditional market research. While this might give you some insight into the recent past, quantitative research and traditional focus groups pale in comparison to getting to know your customers in the context of their lives.

This process starts by loosening the control with which companies interact with customers and the world around them. Rather than trying to control the relationship with customers, one must be a willing and active participant in a dialogue. A company can facilitate this by proactively providing opportunities and resources for this conversation to happen. Within this space, one must go about inviting the right voices or customers to participate in this open, informed process using solid, guiding principles. Most of all, the efforts have to be transparent and human. And, like any other human relationship, there needs to be an effort to evolve them. But the first step is getting out the door of your office. Only then can you begin to experience the exhilaration of co-creating with your customers.

The four chapters of this section offer different perspectives on ways to create an outside-in, co-creative strategy. Rob Bon Durant, Adam DeVito, Michael Perman, and Michael Jager each talk about how they employ holistic, organic methods, allowing their companies to be continually innovative with their customers.

Rob Bon Durant, the director of brand development at Patagonia, typifies many of the people who work there. First, they passionately believe in the vision that the company's owner, Yvon Chouinard, has laid out. Patagonia is more than a company; it is a cause to improve the environment and make the earth a better place to live. Since 1985, the company has pledged 1 percent of sales to the preservation and restoration of the natural environment; it has given away over $18 million in grants to environmental groups worldwide. Who wouldn't want to be part of a company with such a wonderful vision? It's easy to believe in and join a cause that is aligned with your own personal beliefs; that's one of the reasons Patagonia receives thousands of applications for the small number of positions that become available each year!

I wanted to include Rob in the book because he also perfectly represents the "fun hog" aspect of the company. When you've got a compelling corporate vision, people will work hard, but they'll also have fun. Sure, it's easy for the folks at Patagonia to have fun; they work in the outdoor sports industry. But fun can be instilled in any company. The bottom line is that if people are doing something they are passionate about and having fun, chances are they are going to be innovative. Such an environment encourages co-creation with suppliers, customers, and the culture itself. Rob's thoughts on the importance of a broad corporate vision, getting out of the office to spend time with customers, working in an open environment, and last but not least, having fun can give you options for applying some of these principles, with the result of being more innovative.

I've had a couple of different roles in the company. I have a marketing background and was the marketing director for five years and then switched over to the sales and brand development side. Previously, my responsibilities primarily revolved around brand marketing and product marketing, and I worked with our design and development teams on both the product and collateral marketing sides to develop brand messaging and do research and development for line building.

If you look at Patagonia, we have a variety of different sales channels. It's a pretty unique opportunity because we sell online, have our catalogue and mail order business, have our own direct retail stores, and then have a very robust wholesale business.

Open and Fun Environment

As far as our physical environment goes, Patagonia has no offices. We have office buildings, but we have no doors that close except for the conference rooms. Basically, we have an open and very sharing environment, which encourages communication – maybe sometimes too much – but it also absolutely fosters a cooperative type of interaction. The overall theme of the office – that it's very open and fun – happens in a variety of different ways. When you call Patagonia and the machine picks up, it says, "Thanks for calling Patagonia. We're usually open if the surf's not up." So it's very much a "Let my people surf" philosophy.

That's the philosophy that Yvon established 35 years ago when he founded Chouinard Equipment. We were not businesspeople before we came here. We were pretty much climbers and surfers and skiers who found our way through serendipity or otherwise to Patagonia – because Patagonia was an extension of the lifestyle that we all supported and lived. We have a boardroom here, but it's not a typical boardroom – it's actually a board room, filled with surfboards. We have communal bikes with board racks attached that can be taken down to Surfer's Point. We're very much living on the fly in terms of professional versus personal endeavors, but I want to reiterate that we do cover for each other – the work gets done, but it doesn't necessarily get done on a nine to five time-table. We're very nontraditional in that aspect. That in and of itself makes the work environment very unique and very dynamic – if we wind up staying late, it's probably because we took a two-hour lunch to catch a big swell coming in.

> We have a boardroom here, but it's not a typical boardroom – it's actually a board room, filled with surfboards.

Lead, Don't Follow

I can't remember what the statistics are, but we get something like 30,000 applications a year for an average of 30 positions. We don't tend to hire industry professionals or MBAs. It's been a firmly held belief here that it's easier to teach a fun hog to be a businessman than to teach a businessman how to be a fun hog. It's always been the philosophy that we supported, and if we have to do that extra work, we do it willingly because it improves the quality of our professional life. There is no place like Patagonia that I've really run across, especially for a quarter-billion-dollar company – a company this size that can maintain this sort of corporate culture and still stay in the black year after year.

> We ski in it, we climb in it, we rough it up and figure out what's wrong and what needs to be improved and what's perfect.

I think much of our success comes from the fact that we clearly understand and know the product we sell – we live it. When we start our design cycle each season, we don't start it in a boardroom, we don't start it in a conference room under fluorescent lights. We start it in Hawaii if we're designing for the spring and in Colorado or Alaska if we're designing for the winter, and we usually go pretty deep into the backcountry to start that process. We drag everything with us that we've made over the past year. We bring

our athletes – our ambassadors – out with us and we talk about the product. We ski in it, we climb in it, we rough it up, and we figure out what's wrong and what needs to be improved and what's perfect. So we come back with a very clear and rich understanding of what it is that we're up to.

Play and Work Together

Most of us are very close; we have a tendency to work together and play together. My closest friends sit a few feet away from me, and I'm with them all the time – on Fridays we hit the road at four o'clock to spend the weekend climbing or skiing. If we're going skiing for the weekend because of the company that we are, because we supply so many outdoor professionals, I might call a ski patroller and say, "I'm coming up for the weekend" and go out and sweep with him or her in the morning. Basically, what you're getting is a continuation of a lifestyle that's both professional and personal. When I go out skiing with patrollers, it helps me professionally because I'm experiencing what they experience – I'm seeing firsthand the challenges that they put their clothes through and I'm taking that information back. "Okay, we need more durability on the knees" or, "We need to extend a

> On Fridays we hit the road at four o'clock to spend the weekend climbing or skiing.

zipper three inches so it can fit a communication device more appropriately." And all of this happens via the relationship itself – it's not a questionnaire or an online survey; it's very much hands-on, experiential contact.

I think for us, the end of the workday on Friday is the opportunity to really go out and live the lifestyle that we're building professionally during the week. For me, heading out on Friday with a bag full of samples to go climbing is probably the most exciting way I can think of to start a weekend. That may sound kind of corny or trite, but if I'm going to go up there and spend the weekend climbing, I want to try out a bunch of different products and see how they perform – and I want to take that information back to the office and be able to speak from a position of experience, not supposition.

That doesn't mean it feels like I'm working on the weekend. Not at all. We're playing, having fun, and having a great time. Sometimes people tell us to stop talking about work – and we're not talking about financial statements or meeting budgets; we're really talking about whether a particular piece of apparel performed to our expectations on that given climb or that given ski or whatever it might be. For us that's a joy – we're pretty passionate about what we do.

> We're a company that's doing the right thing, that's walking the walk and talking the talk, and everybody looks at us with a fair amount of curiosity.

Take Risks

Everybody's interested in what we're doing, and everybody roots for us. Let's face it – we're a company that's doing the right thing, that's walking the walk and talking the talk, and everybody looks at us with a fair amount of curiosity. We've made significant steps toward swaying the corporate cultures that exist both within and outside of our industry. We do it primarily on the environmental front – ten years ago we made a very strategic decision to move all of our sportswear to organic cotton, which at the time was pretty risky because our sportswear division represented about 60 percent of our sales. And obviously in order to make that switch to organic cotton, we had to subsidize some of our organic cotton farmers so they could afford to grow for us. That raised our retail prices by two or three bucks, which is significant. Our fear was that our customers wouldn't embrace that. But we came together as a company and decided that we were willing to go out of business if it didn't work, because this was important enough to us to make the switch.

You know how the story winds up – not only did our customers support us, but our competition came to us via an invitation and learned how to do it as well. We now have more clothing companies than ever looking at us. If we could only get someone like Gap or Levi's to make the switch to organic cotton, it would destroy the conventional cotton industry – there would be no reason to grow conventionally. So we have an organic cotton symposium every year, and we invite our competition to come to Patagonia to

> We've made significant steps toward swaying the corporate cultures that exist both within and outside of our industry.

cal Mass or Half-Mass Bag

r-bag-inspired Critical Mass and Half-Mass Bags
top sleeve in their main compartment and are
the base and backside to protect contents and
gs standing when set down. The T-strap has a
fixed mesh shoulder pad and a dangle-free web-
nent. The cover flap's roofed and rolled corners
her entry, and the flap pocket accesses along
bag via a water-resistant zip. Two side pockets
mesh, one pleated). Our laptop-loving Vertical
dded compartment for your computer, plenty of
rwork, mesh side pockets for water bottle and cell
r slash pocket on the backside, an inside zip pocket
pocket with a water-resistant zipper. All bags are made from
ier Ballistics nylon and nylon pack cloth, with a polyurethane
'R (Durable water repellent) finish. Imported. Embroidery
ss front pocket zip opening is XXXXXX, total pocket dimen-
XX. Half-Mass front pocket zip opening is XXXXX, total
is are XXXX; Vertical Mass has no pocket on cover flap.
ℓ #48271   *Our retail price* $79.00
computer sleeve, 13.5 x 2" x 11"   **volum** -
14218 • black (159)

learn how to do it. They share with us, and we share all the do's and don'ts of growing and maintaining a sustainable business. We're going to do this – and we're going to keep doing it

Have a Human Face

When people envision Patagonia, I don't want them to envision our logo; I don't want them to envision our type font or even our catalog. I want them to envision a face or a person that they actually met – a living, breathing human being that they had an enjoyable interaction with. That should be the face of Patagonia. That should be the voice of Patagonia. I think that is very much a philosophy that is embraced by all of us.

It's about being passionate about the lifestyle that you're living.

We don't work here for the money; we work here because we're in business to inspire solutions, primarily to environmental crises that are occurring everywhere. The company doesn't exist to make money; the company exists as an environmental action corporate model. We joke all the time that we're this grand experiment, and if we can make this thing work, then hopefully we can be a model to inspire corporate change.

Everybody Can Do It

We're in a sort of unique position working here, because it's easy to be passionate about what we do. But I think that even if you worked for, say, General Mills, it's not so much about being passionate about the cereal; it's about being passionate about the lifestyle that you're living. Obviously, that includes the professional element and existing in a corporate culture that supports creativity, because let's face it, even cereal needs to be creative.

Have Fun

❶ Develop a Broad Corporate Vision – What is your corporate vision? Is it a financially based mission, or one that could be found on the door of any company in the world? (For example, "We provide solutions for our customers.") A corporate vision needs to be big. It needs to have a message that is bigger than just satisfying customers' goals or increasing shareholder value – it's hard for someone in the trenches of the company to get excited about that.

❷ Remove Barriers – Think about how you can develop a more open and sharing office environment. Can you move people together? Focus on creating an environment that increases visibility, accessibility, and interaction.

❸ Be Honest – Patagonia's voice message says that everyone might be out of the office if the surf's good. While that might seem silly to a lot of people, it is honest. Can you and your company be more transparent in an honest and positive way?

❹ Focus on the Work – Great innovation happens at Patagonia. But it doesn't always happen between nine and five. Focus on the work itself, not when it is happening. The fact is that many innovative people work best during nontraditional hours.

❺ Live Your Products – Don't know your products only from the P&L statement or market research data. Go live your products. If you're in the restaurant business, eat all of the meals available on the menu. Then, eat your competitors' selections. Know firsthand how your product does – or doesn't – work.

❻ Spend Time with Teammates – Get to know the people you work with as people. You are on the same team with the goal of innovation, so knowing your teammates more intimately has a real upside. Spend time with them outside of work. Catch dinner; meet their families. But most of all, share experiences that can bring you closer together as a team.

❼ Co-Create with Your Competitors – Innovative companies with a broad vision tend to want to change and influence not only their customers but also the market and industries in which they work. Think about how you could work with competitors and suppliers, creating an environment where a rising tide will increase everyone's fortunes.

_____

_____

_____

_____

_____

_____

_____

_____

_____

_____

_____

_____

_____

_____

_____

Have Fun

Infuse more fun and passion in your work by getting out and seeing your customers. Write down a couple of fun places where your customers hang out. Grab a teammate from work and go interact with your customers. What did you see? What did you learn? Most important, did you have fun?

Resources

1. **Patagonia's Web site:** http://www.patagonia.com.

2. *Serious Play: How the World's Best Companies Simulate to Innovate* by Michael Schrage (Harvard Business School Press). This is a great look at how play generates innovation.

3. **"The Best of the Good"** by Philip Mirvis and Bradley Googins, *Harvard Business Review* 82, no. 12 (December 2004): 20. This short article is an interesting look at the 2003–2004 survey on corporate citizenship.

4. **"The World According to Yvon"** by Monte Burke, *Forbes*, November 26, 2001, 236. A good profile of Yvon Chouinard, the founder of Patagonia sportswear.

5. **"Proven Environmental Commitment Helps Create Committed Customers"** by Jacquelyn Ottman, *Marketing News*, February 2, 1998, 5. Ottman discusses marketing strategies adopted by outdoor clothing firm Patagonia to educate its customers on environmental product attributes and benefits.

6. **The real Patagonia:** www.pbs.org/edens/patagonia. Check out the Patagonia region in Argentina, where Yvon Chouinard found inspiration for his company.

7. **Treehugger:** http://www.treehugger.com/index.php. This cool blog is all about environmental products and issues of sustainable development.

8. Design Green Web site: http://www.designgreen.org. This is an initiative with the mission of transforming business in the U.S. by showing the way toward products that are at once sustainable, innovative, profitable, and able to compete in the global marketplace.

9. *Work Like Your Dog: Fifty Ways to Work Less, Play More, and Earn More* by Matt Weinstein and Luke Barber (Villard). It's all about bringing a more playful attitude to the job!

10. *Fun Works: Creating Places Where People Love to Work* by Leslie Yerkes (Berrett-Koehler Publishers). Yerkes shows how to create an organizational culture that is fun and productive.

11. "Questions and Answers about Fun at Work" by Robert Ford and Frank McLaughlin, *Human Resource Planning* 26, no. 4 (2003): 18. The interesting results of a national e-mail survey of human resource managers in the U.S., as of October 2003, on issues concerning fun working environments.

12. *The Big Book of Motivation Games: Quick, Fun Activities for Energizing People at Work and at Home* by Robert Epstein with Jessica Rogers (McGraw-Hill). Epstein and Rogers create 40 original games and exercises managers can use to motivate their teams and themselves.

To get a handle on the concept of constantly experimenting, I thought I would turn to my friend Adam DeVito. Adam was trained as a chef, starting his career with a classical French cooking apprenticeship. He followed his passion for food by owning restaurants, writing books, and even starting a professional cooking school. This passion also took him into the halls of corporate America as Kraft's executive chef and director of new concept development. Adam is also an experienced strategist and futures planner from the time he spent at Sterling Rice Group as the managing partner. Currently, Adam has been chasing his own entrepreneurial dreams by cofounding and acting as CEO of a toy company, Big Boing Toys. These days he spends a lot of time thinking about how children co-create and innovate.

Adam's ideas about creativity, merging ideas, problem solving, nourishing play, developing curiosity, and creating dialogue are important concepts to think about when allowing a more organic and powerful approach to innovating through the constant experimentation co-creation demands. Adam is one of those rare individuals who empowers others through engagement in dialogue. I am always humbled by my conversations with Adam. He's smart. He's also very caring and thoughtful. When I finish a conversation with Adam, I'm always smiling, and my head is full of optimistic possibilities.

Have you seen the book *Orbiting the Giant Hairball*? If you haven't, it's full of an eclectic combination of pictures and words. It was written by Gordon MacKenzie, the late creative director for Hallmark for 30 years, during Hallmark's most creative period. It's truly a remarkable little book. In fact, I know execs I worked with who bought it for the little anecdotes and stories about being more creative. It's also been a really important book for me in the areas of creativity and innovation. Creativity is like a language that an ancient tribe spoke. As we find ourselves moving through the world at an ever-increasing pace, it's harder to feel a connection to the creative process.

In the first few pages of the book, MacKenzie recounts the experience of going into kindergarten classrooms and asking how many of the kids were artists. Being wide-eyed kindergartners, they all raised their hands. MacKenzie contrasts this with the experience of asking a sixth-grade class the same question; only a couple of kids raised their hands. Unfortunately, our society tells kids they are not artists just because in the picture they've drawn the house is black and the grass is purple. The pressure comes from parents, too. It seems adorable when the kid is in kindergarten, but by the time the kid is in sixth grade, Dad comes home and says, "What's that purple grass? There's no such thing as purple grass." Sooner or later, a kid learns that he or she is not an artist, at least by society's standards. Creativity is the process of kids using their mind's eye to envision the world through their own unique lens. Adults can unwittingly squash this by bringing in their own rational order and enforcing it on children.

This same thing happens in the work environment. It's human nature to put our energy into areas where we feel we have some capacity and ability, but if we're told we're not good at something according to society's norms, we probably won't pursue it. It's a fascinating thing.

The Courage to Create

Most times, normal means fitting in and being linear. I believe that we are here as humans to create, if we have the courage. We have the capacity, but what we often lack is the courage and confidence to create. What I mean by "create" is to develop new ideas and merge new forms of aesthetic. That's really what the human spirit is all about –forming new ideas,

> We have the capacity, but what we often lack is the courage and confidence to create.

merging ideas, blending things out of what exists. It's that ability to think laterally and associatively that really distinguishes us from other animals.

Use Your Imagination

In an ideal world, we would all have a core belief that we're here to create within the context of our jobs, and within the context of our home lives, thinking about problem solving. Problem solving is creating. Any innovation is problem solving. We've lost our nimbleness as a culture as it relates to problem solving, whether it's an innovation solution, a family solution, or dealing with a social dynamic that's uncomfortable with a friend. It's all about your ability to creatively problem-solve. And that's hard to do.

Nourish Play

The company I currently run, Big Boing, is in the business of creating right-brain toys that nourish kids by stimulating creativity. While we make toys, they're not just for kids. They're for everyone. Immersive, self-directed play nourishes and really feeds creativity – it's very open-ended and there are no wrong answers. As soon as you get into a binary yes/no, right/wrong, black/white kind of model – which is where we live – that's inherently not creative. We're so trained in this culture to have opinions about

> Immersive, self-directed play nourishes and really feeds you… it's very open-ended and there are no wrong answers.

everything, when of course the best three words to really stimulate creativity and creative problem solving are "I don't know" or "Tell me more." Using these words creates an environment where solutions will come forth.

Develop Honest Curiosity

If you want to enter a world where magic happens, where opportunities unfold, where things serendipitously reveal themselves, it must start with a question based in honest curiosity. But that's hard in the corporate world. It's hard to find companies that feel like safe environments, where there's a deep sense of belonging. Many companies I've worked for try to create hothouses to become more creative and innovative. Unfortunately, that's hard, because if the hothouse is separate from the organization, there can be resentment. The biggest problem for innovation in big business is the perception that anybody who's doing innovation is not working as hard and is having more fun than everyone else. And, of course, anybody who's ever done innovation work knows that you're actually working harder and you're constantly insecure, thinking that the company is scrutinizing your every move.

> It's hard to find companies that feel like safe environments, where there's a deep sense of belonging.

Never Lose Confidence

In many organizations, your confidence can absolutely be shaken in a matter of a week on the job. Any organization has the ability to take somebody who is inherently a confident person and, through a series of big and small interactions, shake his or her confidence. All it takes is one or two unsuccessful interactions with a couple of key people and you start to say, "Huh?" Before you know it, somebody is looking at you funny, and you're starting to wonder whether that person is thinking of you in some unfair context, and you start to feel a little out of place. You've lost your equilibrium. Your confidence is shot. That's a killer for innovation.

Dialogue versus Judging

Another killer of innovation is the culture that values judging more than dialogue. Well, we've just described two golden rules of large companies. Judging is highly valued because it gets things done, and politics play an important part of the environment as people look for an edge in their career. In this all-too-familiar corporate culture, you don't feel trust or that you're part of a team where you are highly valued and appreciated. But without a deep sense of belonging, creation is difficult. When kids go off and create on their own, they get totally immersed in the act of creating. There is no ego intervention. There is no deep discourse with the ego. It's just pure. They're fully immersed. It's amazing – you can't even reach them. They don't even sense you're there! The alchemy when kids get together can also be amazing. You just can't break in. How do you create an environment where there is a deep sense of belonging and curiosity about the world so that its many layers can percolate up?

> A nurturing environment can lead to a continuous and steady flow of fresh and groundbreaking thinking.

Create the Right Environment

Formal ideation or innovation processes tend to yield more iterative, more derivative, and less novel innovation. It often feels like forcing something down a pipe: "Here's the process, and you're going to innovate against these platforms and then you're going to develop positioning outlines and you're going to put it through a qualitative screen." Real innovation usually emerges from a more organic approach. You've got to let it unfold. Your brain is a muscle; if you let it relax entirely (along with your ego!), it starts to flow with new insights that, in many cases, you're not even aware you have. A nurturing environment, along with the right questions, can lead to a continuous and steady flow of fresh and groundbreaking thinking. There are many ways to "feed" your work environment to nurture innovation. Be a student of the marketplace. Find a large wall or entire room where ideas can be shared broadly. Post media ads, articles, key words, insights, and thoughts – even new products – for all to see. Encourage participation and dialogue. The key is to use the thoughts and ideas as stimuli for the creative process, not as limiting factors.

Take Work Home

Innovation demands that you take your work home. I go home and talk to my wife about ideas. Then she'll start throwing ideas back at me. I'll bring some of those ideas back to the office and share them. Someone will say, "Oh, that's cool," and then we'll all start riffing on the idea from there. It's very much honoring and following the classic ideation rule that there are no bad ideas. What's really happening is we're just allowing baby ideas to develop more fully before judging them.

Context

Another important factor in being innovative is your frame of reference. A lot of people get stuck in the trap of trying to create something that is really innovative, something that doesn't exist in the world today. But the truth is that an innovation that is really supercreative, that has resonance and power plus the ability to do extremely well in the marketplace, is already part of a clear set of products that already exists. In other words, they have a clear context, but there's something novel about the way that an innovation is being thought about that really shifts the paradigm.

Without a context, an innovation lacks a cord of familiarity or a connection point for consumers.

In some situations, someone will come forth and say, "I've got something really amazing." In their mind it's a huge idea, but when they start to explain it, nobody in the room understands what they're talking about. It might be a great idea, but it will never sell if people, especially customers, don't have a context for it. If you are going to innovate effectively, you have to provide the frame. That's one of the least-understood things about innovation – people think it's all about such unbridled creativity.

Sometimes, enormous leaps and bounds are just too enormous. Without a context, an innovation lacks a cord of familiarity or a connection point for consumers. Our society today is moving pretty fast. People need to have an immediate and clear connection or familiarity with something. However, it is important to also mention that occasionally there are new inventions or shifts in the marketplace that aren't anticipated and that have a huge impact, literally changing the way we see the world. Every time there's one of those major transformational shifts, there's an opportunity to really look at the world differently. The Internet and 9/11 are prime examples. Futures and scenario planning are tools to help anticipate this level of step-change that literally shifts the frame.

Transformation

There are transformational things, big and small, happening around us constantly. That's why we have to be more innovative. Only by staying connected and having the courage to be a kindergartner, drawing black houses and purple grass, will companies be able to survive and thrive. Think of the company as a community of people – a living organism with a collective unconscious. This collective unconscious is the most fertile way to brainstorm with your team and your customers. True innovation is really about aligning new ideas to plausible outcomes in the marketplace. It's also about timing. So many really wonderful innovations miss their timing window. To survive in these times, you have to connect with people who live completely outside of your business. The people who have a fresh eye, the true agnostics, will be the people who will literally rock your world.

It's harder than ever before to nurture innovation within and around us. Our racing minds jump in and tell us what we think we should expect of ourselves. Striving for money and material things really get in the way, too. If we're able to free ourselves of those expectations and social constructs, it allows us to be much more immersed in the act of living and letting things unfold. Then you realize that in fact you are doing exactly what you should be doing. To innovate successfully, you have to understand some of these basic tenets about human potential, about interaction, dynamics, and communication, and about how fragile the environment really is that fosters a spirit of innovation and creative problem solving.

> The people who have a fresh eye, the true agnostics, will be the people who will literally rock your world.

Tools

Constantly Experiment

❶ Find a Creative Outlet – Become a part-time artist. Take up a hobby that pushes your ability to draw outside the lines; try drawing, photography, quilting, or anything else that might get your creative juices flowing. All of these activities encourage learning through failure and experimentation.

❷ Keep a Journal – Many of the innovative people I know keep a detailed journal of their experiences that they can draw on again and again to help them be more innovative. Some people like to write in their journal, others draw, while others collect interesting artifacts from life's journey.

❸ Spend Time with Kids – Find a way to explore co-creation and build more confidence to experiment by spending time with kids. Whether it's your own kids or through a program such as Big Brothers and Big Sisters, by allowing yourself to look at the world through children's eyes, you will be better able to follow their example.

❹ Be More Intuitive – Business, by its very nature, is about the discipline of repeating something very well. Try incorporating intuition in your work by telling more stories, encouraging others to be intuitive, and listening more.

❺ Take Your Work Home – If you've got a big issue that's a roadblock for being innovative, solicit feedback from your friends and family. By taking a more holistic approach to problem solving, more interesting solutions will emerge.

❻ Practice Creativity – When you're working on a project, think about the craziest solution to a problem. What would happen if you had no constraints in co-creating a new product with your customers? How would the product or service be different?

❼ Nourish Play – You can be more innovative by nourishing play with your team. Instead of getting locked down in another meeting trying to divine a solution to a problem, experiment by playing. You could do this by simply changing the context of the meeting or engaging the group in an improv game.

_____

_____

_____

_____

_____

_____

_____

_____

_____

_____

_____

_____

_____

_____

Constantly Experiment

Think about your own creativity. Has it been stifled? Draw a picture of your customer with all the passion of a kindergartner.

Resources

1. Big Bang Ideas Web site: http://www.bigbangideas.com. Big Bang is the parent company of Big Boing Toys: http://www.bigboing.com.

2. *Orbiting the Giant Hairball: A Corporate Fool's Guide to Surviving with Grace* by Gordon MacKenzie (Penguin Putnam). Adam enthusiastically endorses this book in the interview – check it out.

3. *Jamming: The Art and Discipline of Business Creativity* by John Kao (Harper Business). Kao has interesting thoughts about mixing right- and left-brain activities to be creative.

4. *Creating Minds: An Anatomy of Creativity Seen Through the Lives of Freud, Einstein, Picasso, Stravinsky, Eliot, Graham, and Gandhi* by Howard Gardner (Basic Books). I always love trying to understand the masters.

5. *Creativity: Flow and the Psychology of Discovery and Invention* by Mihaly Csikszentmihalyi (Harper Perennial). A good look at how the mind works with creativity.

6. *If Life Is a Game, How Come I'm Not Having Fun? A Guide to Life's Challenges* by Paul Brenner (State University of New York Press). Brenner, an analyst at the U.S. Department of Commerce, conceptualizes economic, political, social, and spiritual pursuits in terms of role-playing and argues that this perspective can contribute to people's happiness as well as to social well-being.

7. *The 100 Greatest Business Ideas of All Time* by Ken Langdon (Oxford: Capstone). Nothing like a little inspiration.

8. *The Art of Innovation: Lessons in Creativity from IDEO, America's Leading Design Firm* by Tom Kelley (Doubleday). There's a lot to learn from great companies like IDEO.

9. Bruce Mau's Web site: http://www.brucemaudesign.com
and http://www.massivechange.com. Mau is another designer
with a broad vision of change, culture, and creativity.

10. *The Artist's Way: A Spiritual Path to Higher Creativity*
by Julia Cameron (Jeremy P. Tarcher). Practice makes
perfect.

11. *Ideation: The Birth and Death of Ideas* by Douglas
Graham and Thomas T. Bachman (John Wiley & Sons). It's
always good to remember how to ideate.

12. *Breakthrough Creativity: Achieving Top Performance
Using the Eight Creative Talents* by Lynne C. Levesque
(Davies-Black). This is a good look at the application of the
Myers-Briggs typology.

13. *Adaptors and Innovators: Styles of Creativity and
Problem Solving* edited by M. J. Kirton (London: Routledge).
Kirton is known for his adaptors/innovators theoretical model
for explaining creativity.

**14. "Another Look at Creativity Styles: Reporting on
Research and a New Question"**: http://www.tri-network.com/
reading_corner/kaimbti.html. An overview of Kirton's creativity
model of adaptors/innovators and the Myers-Briggs typology.

15. Myers-Briggs Type Indicator: http://skepdic.com/
myersb.html. A brief summary of the Myers-Briggs type
indicator.

16. The Blue Man Group Web site: http://www.blueman.com.
These guys are great. They are a fun, creative trio of
performers who use ordinary objects in unexpected,
innovative ways.

The idea of being customer inspired without becoming customer reliant has been a very hot topic over the last few months on BrandShift, a blog I coedit. One interesting comment from a designer was: "Sure, good designers listen and observe users as a source of inspiration for the design process, but when you start doing what GM did with the new 'baby' Hummer and force your skilled, highly trained designers to change the visceral elements of their designs based on the feedback of visually uneducated critics, well, the train bound for Mediocrityville has already left the station."

As you can see, there is a constant tension between the idea of being customer reliant and being customer inspired. The ultimate goal is to co-create with customers in a way that exceeds their expectations. This idea is perfectly expressed by Michael Jager, creative director of Jager Di Paola Kemp, a renowned design firm based in Burlington, Vermont. Jager provides an interesting and inspired look at this dynamic between reliance and inspiration in the world of co-creation. His viewpoint comes from participating in the creation of the Burton Snowboard brand and being deeply connected with youth culture. Michael's concepts of differentiation, progression, creating a culture inside your company that mirrors your customers' culture, companies as inspired protagonists, and the importance of always learning are important ideas that are seeping from the confines of individual sports like skateboarding to the boardrooms of the world's most progressive companies.

Inspiration

To me the essence of leading, following, or nurturing a culture of innovation starts with the depth of your belief in differentiation and the importance of differentiation. What drives it? Is it your desire for progression, something that you need to do to be successful as a brand, as a consumer product, or as an individual? It goes back to a respect for differentiation. It means being willing to take that risk and not be afraid of it but also finding pleasure and desiring progression. The idea of progression is what I've used to help guide my thinking. To me, having a commodified existence is pretty painful and useless. People and companies that are followers instead of leaders don't necessarily always stay on the path to commodification. Certainly, it's not a very exciting place. You can be a second-place company following innovations and tweaking other people's ideas and remain in a place beyond commodity, but I don't want to be one of those people nor do I want to work for a culture like that. It's far more interesting to become an inspired protagonist in a market. And by taking that position, you need to be deeply connected to the culture that your products exist in and the people who use them yet rely on your intuition about where things will be.

Differentiation and Progression

For me, the belief in differentiation and progression is born out of growing up in the individualist sports scene. There is a degree of competitiveness. But when skaters are dropping into a half-pipe or pool, progression is a much better description than competition. In its purest sense, progression is a really beautiful thing because it's about feeding off the human energy that drives other people to push themselves further. It's just this vibe that creates innovation and thinking. This idea of progression is part of what the youth culture of this generation has brought into the global business culture. The essence of progression is the desire for differentiation. Companies need to breed that into their relationship with customers. It's about a dialogue. When you really get the subtle meanings of this dialogue, you can progress the conversation and even lead it.

> The essence of progression is the desire for differentiation.

If you're going to create things that really move the needle in an innovative way and get the added benefit of buzz from the energy and excitement for your product in the culture, then people need to see how provocative the change really is. To be innovative today you have to lead your customers.

Dynamic Dialogue

That means you need to be in the dialogue with your customers and the culture. It's not observation alone; it's an ongoing, dynamic dialogue. One of the things that has really changed since I started JDK is that the idea of a dynamic dialogue, born out of sports like mountain biking and snowboarding, has seeped into the general culture. The dynamics of how a company and its customers interact have changed. Information sharing, including the power of music in the digital realm, has changed the amount and the scale of the dynamics on the dialogue. The dynamics have gotten so diverse.

> The dynamics of how a company and its customers interact have changed.

It's important to create a very diverse culture inside your company as well, because the dialogue in the culture is so diverse. You need to have multiple synapses firing at the same time. It's very easy to get trapped by the narrow focus on the category that you're in; it's very hard to comprehend everything that is going on and use that information. However, you can't stop there – the contexts in which consumers are judging your innovations and ideas are so diverse that you are forced to understand a much broader spectrum of the culture.

As an example, the design team for the Mini Cooper had to have a very clear understanding that they were being judged in the context of a larger cultural market that included, say, the furniture industry and dwelling trends. They needed to understand what was happening in the fashion industry as well. They were therefore able to make alignments with people like Puma, when they realized that apparel needed to be part of the vernacular that they were creating. They understood that people's relationships to things like the iPod play an important role in people's lives. So all that seemed to really inform what they did when they created the design of the Mini, internally and externally: the form, the colors, the custom combinations, the touch and feel, the writing of the manuals, and the fact that they did a DVD/technical manual versus just a printed manual. They understood that the context was vast and their audience was absolutely connected in all those places.

In fact, in one of our projects, we started documenting the process of creating an innovation and the dialogue we had with the culture. We felt that documenting the process was another way to connect deeper with the customers, to reflect who they were and to recruit talent who could show what their culture was about. So it was a catalyst for a project that will have a profound effect.

> In one of our projects, we started documenting the process of creating an innovation and the dialogue we had with the culture.

Be an Inspired Protagonist

One of our clients, Burton, is still a leading, powerful brand after many years in the whole culture of snowboarding. A major reason for this is because they helped establish and create the sport. They were really the protagonists that pulled the culture forward; they helped to define it. Working in the beginning with that audience, it was really clear that customers were hungry for more information. They wanted to keep the sport moving and progressing. It was a cause, an idea; not just great, unique products.

We were learning about how far we could push that radical evolution and change, how constant it should be, and we started to develop ideas around the concept that Burton was really a "living brand." This change in perspective helped when the company went from being a small rebel brand to becoming the antithesis of that – the biggest snowboard brand. Snowboarders started looking at Burton and thinking the company was a big corporate giant, and other, smaller brands tried to leverage that against them, stating their role as "specialized" in the scene. So in talking to the audience, Burton had to enter the dialogue as being focused, pure, and authentic. That meant, for one, ensuring that every single ad was unique; we never ran an ad more than once. We became very nimble. We also ended up having 30 to 40 different logos operating at once. We broke every traditional rule of corporate identity.

One of the more innovative things we did in marketing was an ad campaign similar to a chain letter to the audience. There was messaging and imaging that leapt from one ad to the next so customers could connect this chain together. At the end of the year, all the key voices in the market were following the campaign and could connect this chain together. It was like a 120-foot-long message from Burton that

We broke every traditional rule of corporate identity.

linked all this information and imagery together. It's great; people have collected all these ads. This idea was completely developed from the idea of being in a dialogue with the audience.

Create an Eclectic Culture

We try to have a culture that is open to people. We invite them to be out in the market. The people we have at JDK are part of the audience. We also respect the learning. We respect that it's diverse; the designers, the account directors, and strategists all need to see film, see architecture, maybe go to parties where they might not feel comfortable. A lot of that is just creating a culture where it's okay to hang out. In a field like design, which is very intense, demanding, and time-consuming on a service level, this isn't very easy for people – but it's critical. We also create an environment where the culture comes to us at the office. We have a gallery downstairs where we run all kinds of unique and diverse-discipline work, so there are openings and experiments all the time. We also have a skateboard ramp in the basement that is open to anybody we might want to invite to come hang out and skate with us, whether it's clients, kids in the area, pro riders, or people visiting the gallery. We're even thinking about opening a café in the front of our building – once again, based on the objective of establishing dialogue.

The designers, the account directors, and strategists all need to see film, see architecture, maybe go to parties where they might not feel comfortable.

Cross-Fertilization

We want to create a spot where people can create an experience, talk and meet each other, and learn and share. When the surrealist movement happened in

Paris in the 1920s and 1930s, everything came together: literature, photography, art, and sculpture. Everybody in the scene was having a very deep dialogue. They were colliding together and challenging everything. This is the scene and the dream that changes everything.

Cross-fertilization and free association are important. That's why it's important to get out in the culture and explore. Travel. Go to Iceland or New Zealand and hang out with shepherds. If you want to learn something about warmth and layering, go to those places. You can find things. Unless you're out there learning and gathering information in a lot of diverse places, it's just not possible to be innovative. This is not easy to accomplish, but it's key to discovery and differentiation.

This certainly is important in design, but I think it applies to anybody. I can learn from anything, whether it's learning from my kids or a walk in the woods, trail running, going to a museum or a monster truck rally; whatever it is. I think there's something to be learned from every single thing I do. I really don't find that much to be boring; there's always something more to learn. I am just hungry for information. The biggest frustration I have is that there are not 40 hours in a day to gather more and document more. It's almost as though I'm afraid of what I'm missing; I wonder if I could find new color combinations if only I could get out in the woods more, for example.

I keep ideas and information in journals. I also shoot a lot of photography and have a huge file I call "Stuff I like" that's kept in several binders with

Unless you're out there learning and gathering information in a lot of diverse places, it's just not possible to be innovative.

acetate envelopes. I've gathered feathers and rocks, photos, printed pieces, you name it. There is even some scary, weird stuff in there. I actually have a collection of dead birds I keep in my freezer. Years ago, I found a dead robin by the side of the road that had been hit by a car. There was no damage to the body at all. I remember thinking to myself, This is so beautiful. Since then I've managed to collect about a dozen dead birds; I shoot photos of them. They're beautiful and really inspiring. I'm like this little soul collector, I guess.

> That's what brilliant teachers do.... they act as inspired protagonists of unique perspectives.

Teaching and Learning

When people are able to practice and help create a culture of innovation, they become teachers. The greatest teachers have diverse knowledge. Because of this, they reach a diverse audience. I often find that people are so close to their category that they can't see it anymore. They're so dense with information that if someone can just say, "Well, okay. Let's put an apple on the table and talk about its relationship to this pencil," all of a sudden people will see something new. That's what brilliant teachers always do.... they act as inspired protagonists of unique perspectives.

❶ Differentiation – When you are listening to your customers, think about how you can make your product or service different. Michael's example of how Burton used several logos at once to differentiate its brand among many customers is a great example of being customer inspired. Burton took a nontraditional path to having a closer relationship with each of its customer groups. What can you do to infuse differentiation as you innovate?

❷ Progression – It's important to think about evolution versus revolution. As an example, one of the things that impresses me most about the iPod is not its brilliant revolution but the rapid progression of both the iPod and related products like iTunes. Customers stay engaged with this innovation progression.

❸ Become an Inspired Protagonist – Many iconic brands such as Nike and Virgin have inspired customers by pushing against the establishment, asking the hard questions, and overturning the status quo. How can your company become an inspired protagonist in the market you serve? How can your team act as an inspired protagonist within your company? Becoming an inspired protagonist will engender a following of fans, all willing to participate in co-creation.

❹ Deepen Your Connections – Michael talks about how he deepens the connection with his customers by hiring people who want to interact with them. They want to be a part of and explore their customers' lives because, in many cases, they *are* the customers. Do you have people inside your company who are the customers?

❺ Create a Dynamic Dialogue – Think about how you interact with your customers. Is it dynamic? Is there a spirit of give and take, of listening and learning, on both sides of the table? Dialogue is a very difficult thing to achieve, but it is the basis of co-creation.

❻ Mirror Your Customer's Culture – Yvon Chouinard, the founder of Patagonia, recently finished his long-awaited biography. Instead of a traditional biography, the book evolved into a business book, *Let My People Surf*. In it, he discusses how employees at Patagonia work hard but are strongly encouraged (and given the time) to pursue their passions, which usually means getting out and doing outdoor sports with their customers. Can you create a culture on your team or in your company that more closely mirrors your customers' culture?

❼ Cross-Fertilize – The contexts of your customers' lives are vast. You need to understand their lives as a whole. One way to do that is to find noncompetitive companies that serve the same customers and share insights and inspirations with them. Are there projects you can work on together with mutual benefits?

Interaction

_____

_____

_____

_____

_____

_____

_____

_____

_____

_____

_____

_____

_____

Be Customer Inspired, Not Reliant

Think about how your company relates to its customers. Are you customer inspired or reliant? Write down three ways that you could progress your current relationship with your customers and become an inspired protagonist. Can you take a stand on a worthy but controversial cause that could differentiate you in the marketplace?

Be Customer Inspired, Not Reliant

1. Jager Di Paola Kemp's Web site: http://www.jdk.com.

2. *Creativity at Work: Developing the Right Practices to Make Innovation Happen* by Jeffrey T. DeGraff and Katherine A. Lawrence (Jossey-Bass). A good place to gain knowledge about creativity.

3. "Building Leadership Brands by Design" by Jerome Kathman, *Brandweek*, December 1, 2003. A good article that highlights the importance of the commitment to innovation.

4. Reputation Institute: http://www.reputationinstitute.com/main/home_base.php. A great place to gain knowledge about corporate reputations, their management, measurement, and valuation.

5. "American Marketers Should Relearn the Benefit of Taking Risks" by Jonah Bloom, *Advertising Age*, February 16, 2004. A great article on why risk aversion doesn't work.

6. "When to Put the Brakes on Learning" by J. Stuart Bunderson and Kathleen M. Sutcliffe, *Harvard Business Review*, February 2003. The article examines how much management teams should focus on learning.

7. "When Your Culture Needs a Makeover" by Carol Lavin Bernick, *Harvard Business Review*, June 2001. Bernick writes an interesting piece on how to know when your company is in need of a cultural reinvention and what to do about it.

8. *A New Brand World: 8 Principles for Achieving Brand Leadership in the 21st Century* by Scott Bedbury (Viking). Scott has a great take on the whole question of differentiation.

9. "No Risk, No Reward" by Keith H. Hammonds, *Fast Company*, April 2002. This article is a good exploration of lessons learned by people and organizations on taking risks in business.

10. *Beyond Rules in Society and Business* by Verner C. Petersen (E. Elgar Publications). This is an interesting read on the moral and ethical aspects of business and management.

11. *Creating the Multicultural Organization: A Strategy for Capturing the Power of Diversity* by Taylor Cox (Jossey-Bass). A good resource to think about the issues of cultural diversity.

12. Artcyclopedia.com: http://www.artcyclopedia.com/history/surrealism.html. This is a good resource on the history of surrealism.

13. The MadSci Network: http://www.madsci.org. Check out what's happening on this interesting teaching site, especially the Surrealism Compliment Generator: http://www.madsci.org/cgi-bin/cgiwrap/~lynn/jardin/SCG. Very funny.

14. Product Development and Management Association: www.pdma.org. PDMA is always a valuable innovation resource.

15. "The Rise of the Creative Consumer," *Economist*, March 12, 2005, 59. Another great article about how and why smart companies are harnessing the creativity of their customers.

16. *Democratizing Innovation* by Eric Von Hippel (MIT Press). Eric has written a great book about involving customers in innovation.

One of my favorite clients is Michael Perman, senior director of consumer insights at Levi Strauss & Co. He makes me think. He wants to know more. And most of all, he wants to immerse himself in the lives of his customers. When Michael used to work in the food industry, he would occasionally go out and ride with the independent truck drivers who delivered his products to convenience stores. Michael says, "Riding in the truck and being in the factory were a couple of places to have points of contact with reality." Michael has had an interesting journey in his career, starting in the food industry, owning his own marketing firm, and working in his current role at Levi's.

Michael is all about immersion, whether it's riding along in a delivery truck or checking out a customer's closet. We can all learn a great deal from Michael about the power of firsthand experience in having a dialogue with our customers.

Michael's thoughts regarding getting to know your customers better, inspirations that drive design principles, how to explore your environment, getting down on the individual level of a customer, contextualizing customers' lives to find inspiration, and escaping the focus group trap are wonderful examples of how to break out of the routine of sitting in an office and analyzing data. Instead, finding powerful insights by immersing yourself in the customer culture not only fuels innovation through inspiration, it also lays a foundation for further co-creation.

Michael shows that even within a large organization with a great deal of its own innovation heritage, you can, as an individual, seek a new path and add something substantial to the innovation dialogue through immersion.

Inspiration

So the real question is, how does getting into the lives of customers help us be more innovative at any level? I think at the heart of our design principles at Levi's are values that emerge from cultural and consumer-driven inspiration. It's a pathway that's been baked into the culture of the company. Finding deep cultural inspirations by really getting to know people extensively, as people, enables us to understand the values that drive their behavior, which will lead to design principles. From those design principles emerge great products and great marketing ideas.

For instance, our work in 2003 identified four major sea changes. One is called "The appearance of readiness," the second is called "Attitude trumps age," the third is called "Consumer power play," and finally, "General ADD." The first one, the appearance of readiness, was about people's desire to put on personas that make them feel like they're ready for a certain activity. They wanted to feel like they were ready to embrace the world around them, including the problems, opportunities, frustrations, and transformations relevant to them.

At the time we were exploring these issues, the United States entered the war in Iraq. A lot of disengagement by American consumers seemed to be brewing. There was also a lot of distrust of society – you know, you can't trust priests, you can't trust Martha Stewart, you can't trust corporations and government. There was an awareness that you're on your own and need to take care of yourself. We discovered people thinking that they'd feel better if they put on some sort of a persona to help get them through this time of uncertainty. An example of this would be the Hummer and the proliferation of SUVs. Do you know how many people who drive SUVs actually use them for the intended purpose?

Like many other products in society, SUVs are overengineered because they can be. This inspiration is what led us to develop many products in the work wear category. When I talk about work wear, I'm not talking about professional grade work wear. It's not designed for welders or gardeners. Instead, work wear includes cargo and carpenter pants with hidden pockets. These pants include all sorts of design features to give that "ready for anything" look. Surprisingly, even in our women's apparel line we developed products that were service oriented, inspired by the functionality of overnight express delivery drivers and policewomen. The key was to create apparel that let the customers give the impression they were providing some sort of service to the world. Another thing we found in our exploration in 2003 was the emergence of active wear inspired by yoga. Everyone may not necessarily be doing yoga, but still wants to look ready for it.

Finding deep cultural inspirations by really getting to know people extensively, as people, enables you to understand the values that drive their behavior.

Looking for Control

In these uncertain times, people want to be more in control and more in charge of the world around them. To gain this control, there is a shift from consumption to creation. Certainly, this is clearly reflected in the number of television shows like *Extreme Makeover* and *Pimp My Ride*. These shows are all about making transformations in your life. What I find interesting is that these shows are about the viewers and not about a star. It's not about something you buy ready-made; it's about things that you have a part in creating. The idea is that everyone can be a creator. These shows reflect Richard Florida's point of view in his book *The Rise of the Creative Class* that a lot of people want to have a sense of creation rather than a sense of buying more packaged stuff. A lot of the insights we derive from our explorations include people saying, for example, "I go to a department store, and I see an enormous display of shirts that all look the same. I'm just overwhelmed and uninspired by that." That has led us to produce jeans for women with some real personal touches, including embroidery, little fabric inlays, and things that have a more handcrafted feel to them.

> A lot of people want to have a sense of creation rather than a sense of buying more packaged stuff.

Transparency and Authenticity

We also find there's an increased desire from consumers for more corporate transparency and more authenticity. That's good for Levi's. But that brings up the point that it's a lot easier to be able to ride a cultural shift than it is to fight it. By immersing ourselves and understanding this cultural shift, we could really leverage Levi's authenticity. This was reflected in our products and advertising as well, focusing on individuals who have humble but interesting lives – they are not movie stars or models. These people are all about being themselves, and there's something very authentic and personal about that. It's all about personal expression, being yourself, your ultimate comfort – and for Levi's, we have a jean that works for you.

One-to-One

Today, we get out and try to understand the world by getting down to the individual level. In the past, we looked at markets really broadly. Now there are a lot more questions being asked about real people. We may have an idea for a product or marketing initiative we want to appeal to men, but there are a hundred million of them. Instead of trying to understand them all, what we try to do is contextualize their lives to find inspiration. It's important to boil inspiration down to a practical, individual level. It's interesting; I hear more people talking in those terms around the company now – designers, merchandisers, and marketing people. They are starting to talk more about the importance of leveraging an inspiration and staying as focused as possible.

Many companies do this by creating theoretical or fake personas of their typical customer. But it's much

> It's important to boil inspiration down to a practical, individual level.

more important to get out, immerse yourself in your customers' lives, and understand the real personas of your customers.

Using Technology
Today it's easier to get people engaged with the immersion process through technology. It doesn't matter how many employees you have around the world. A lot more people can now get involved with the inspiration. Technology is contributing to that.

Ride Along
In my earlier life working for a food company, I'd immerse myself by riding in the distributor's truck. I don't think people ride the trucks as much any more. Most companies have downsized so much that people don't ever get out of their offices. Riding in the truck is a bit of a metaphor, but there's a kind of literal importance to it because the towns you go to and people you meet understand the behind-the-scenes reality. You have to have your own taste of this reality. You can't replicate it. I rode in the truck with what they call candy/tobacco jobbers. These guys sell cigarettes, candy, and beef jerky, and they go to all of the little stores everywhere and deliver their goods. When you're immersing yourself at this level, you see a different reality. You never forget the way the warehouse smells. It's a combination of tobacco, chocolate, and smoked meat in one warehouse, a very distinctive fragrance that's really kind of pleasant. It's the scent of reality.

How many managers get out there and spend time with their customers?

I was recently at an innovation conference in New York and one of the speakers said something that stayed with me. He thought it was very interesting that the people in hotels who are supposed to have the greatest amount of contact with consumers are more likely to be found in the back office than in a place to connect with customers. If you think of the least customer-facing person in the hotel, it's the front desk supervisor, who tends to be in the back of the room. There's something very ironic about that. Most companies suffer from the same problem. How many managers get out there and spend time with their customers? They'd be better off if they got out and rode in a truck every once in a while.

Fewer Focus Groups

Lots of companies rely too heavily on focus groups. You've got to break down the two-way mirror, break the fourth wall. There are a lot of tools and techniques for making it happen, but there's a real art to it also. I always look forward to getting out in the field to be able to do that sort of thing, and I'm frustrated if I find myself in a position where we're still conducting interviews and not having discussions.

> You've got to break down the two-way mirror, break the fourth wall.

I've been at Levi Strauss & Co. for four years and I still need to get out more. I really want to get to one of our factories and make my own pair of jeans. And there's a cotton farmer out there somewhere who makes the cotton that we use to make our jeans – I want to meet him.

Tools

Immerse Yourself

❶ Know the Context of the Situation – So many times when we explore our customers' opinions – usually through the use of focus groups – we have a difficult time understanding the context of their lives. It is important to immerse yourself in the lives of your customers if you truly want to understand them. Do they watch *Survivor*, take public transportation, go to the ballet? You should as well.

❷ Be a Better Listener – Good listening is hard. It's too easy to have a conversation and listen only for the proper time to add your two-cents' worth. Slow down and really concentrate on what others say. They might be good co-creative participants. Also, remember that listening needs to be practiced with all of your senses; 70 percent of all communication is nonverbal. Such listening will give you more confidence to use your intuition when thinking about innovation.

❸ Rely on Experience – The only way to become good at immersing yourself in the lives of your customers is to do it. You've got to take that first step. Ask the first dumb question. The more experience you have doing so, the easier immersion becomes.

❹ Get Out into the Culture – The San Francisco Museum of Modern Art recently installed a Levi's research report into its permanent collection. Michael frequently takes people from Levi's over to the museum to check it out. In the process, people get exposed to all kinds of culture. How can you expose your team members to other cultures that might have a profound influence on their work?

❺ Identify Key Customer Voices – When you are exploring a way to immerse yourself with your customers, it is essential to identify opinion leaders. If you are thinking about spending time with a potential subject, ask about the influential people in their life. This cuts to the core of the issue.

❻ Focus on Firsthand Experiences – It's much easier to sit behind your desk reading quantitative data or behind a one-way mirror in a focus group facility, but your learning is limited. Even watching a well-constructed video of an immersion is no substitute for the real thing. You've got to get out there and interact with your customers, listening and observing firsthand.

❼ See the Whole Picture – When you do start learning through immersion, it's easy to overemphasize or become obsessed with the strategic question at hand. Stop. Take a deep breath and look around. Getting the whole picture is an important aspect of really understanding a customer's story.

❽ Be Subjective – There is no such thing as objectivity, so forget about it. Instead, think about what biases and agendas you do have and how they might affect what you hear and see. By practicing immersion more, you'll start to notice the patterns you bring to your participation.

_____

_____

_____

_____

_____

_____

_____

_____

_____

_____

_____

_____

_____

_____

_____

Immerse Yourself

Plan a fun immersion opportunity with your customers. Where could you go? To a bar, a Laundromat? Take your camera. When you get back, write down what you learned. What was hard? What was fun? What will you do next time?

Immerse Yourself

1. Levi Strauss & Co. Web site: http://www.levi.com.

2. *The Rise of the Creative Class and How It's Transforming Work, Leisure, Community and Everyday Life* by Richard Florida (Basic Books). Florida captures the sea change of how people are seeking their own path.

3. *The Cultural Creatives: How 50 Million People Are Changing the World* by Paul H. Ray and Sherry Ruth Anderson (Harmony Books): www.culturalcreatives.org/home.html. An interesting look at a big part of the consumer population.

4. *The Tipping Point: How Little Things Can Make a Big Difference* by Malcolm Gladwell (Back Bay Books). Remember that some voices are more important than others.

5. *The Grace of Great Things: Creativity and Innovation* by Robert Grudin (Ticknor & Fields). Grudin has produced a great primer on immersing yourself in creativity.

6. *How Designers Think: The Design Process Demystified* by Bryan Lawson (Architectural Press). A great survey of how designers connect and immerse themselves in the world.

7. *On Creativity* by David Bohm (Routledge). Bohm is always an essential read.

8. *This Is a Pair of Levi's Jeans: The Official History of the Levi's Brand* by Lynn Downey, Jill Novack Lynch, and Kathleen McDonough (Gingko Press). This book gives some context to Michael's thoughts.

9. *A Century of American Icons: 100 Products and Slogans from the 20th-Century Consumer Culture* by Mary Cross (Greenwood Press). A good history of 20th-century American consumer culture.

10. Complaints.com: http://www.complaints.com. A great database of personal, firsthand consumer experiences with products and services.

11. "The Rules of Reality" by Andy Davidson, *Brand Strategy*, November 2004, 8. Davidson talks about the need for companies to focus on authenticity.

12. "Marketing to Generation®" by Stephen Brown, *Harvard Business Review*, June 2003, 16. A good look at today's marketing-savvy consumers.

The Culture

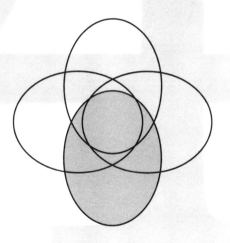

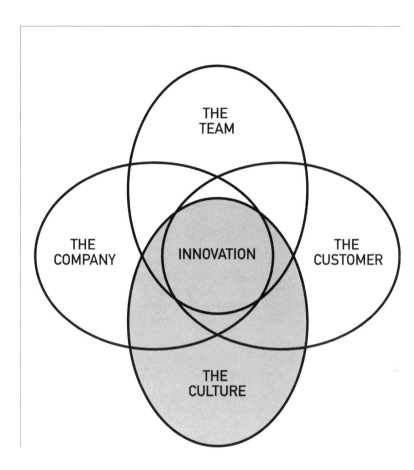

When I talk about culture, I am talking about it in a broad sense, including cultural issues, competitors, retailers, suppliers, the political environment, and so on. Unless you take the time to understand the culture in which you and your customers exist, you will not be able to understand the context of your efforts. Really understanding the culture is a hard job. It means finding new ways to connect not just to your customers but also to the world, in general, and discover how your innovation efforts fit into this broader context.

The four chapters in this section, "Develop New Relationships," "Let the Culture Create Itself," "Build a Community," and "Develop New Ways to Connect," will challenge your notion of connecting with your culture and inspire you to use the tools provided to find new and more intimate ways to connect with the world around you.

It's very easy to become too tactical in trying to understand the stories from the culture. Many people want to immediately figure out how an innovation might be used. The real key to understanding the culture is to soften your focus and proceed slowly enough to understand the subtle context of the culture. Barney Feinblum, Pat Keane, Jake McKee, and Christine Halvorson are all on the cutting edge of connecting with the culture and will provide you with widened vision on how you might apply some new tools to form a foundation of co-creating innovation.

Most people who work in the natural foods business know Barney Feinblum. He has become an icon in the industry, having spent the past quarter of a century either starting or investing in 25 different companies. Barney got his start working for the herbal tea brand Celestial Seasonings. From there he went on to serve as president and CEO of Horizon Organic Dairy, creating the leading organic food brand in the United States. Currently, he is the CEO of Organic Vintners.

One of the things I really admire about Barney is his ability to find unique ways of working with suppliers. He has literally been on the ground, working with farmers and dairies to understand and comply with basic processes to meet his companies' standards. As a consumer, I remember when Horizon started. At the time, the word *organic* was being defined in several different ways. One of Barney's strategies was to give solid meaning to organic in the dairy business. That meant not only defining the word but co-creating innovative practices with suppliers to make sure that Horizon could guarantee its customers the quality they wanted.

In an effort to be more innovative, all of us can work with our suppliers in new ways. Barney's thoughts about leveraging relationships with suppliers – not reinventing the wheel – working with smaller suppliers, getting out with suppliers, and looking at smaller niches are all important ideas when thinking about new ways to co-create.

One of my first jobs out of college was working for Samsonite as a production manager on the assembly lines. I started my career at Celestial Seasonings when my wife saw an ad in the paper about Celestial looking for a production manager. I took two-thirds the salary I was then making to go to work for them. I remember I wore a coat and tie to the job interview, even though I knew a little bit about that company. I was greeted by the secretary, who lived in a teepee up in Four Mile Canyon outside of Boulder, Colorado. She walked me up to the personnel director's office. He was sitting there in shorts and a T-shirt, and I thought, *This is the place for me.* I was the only one who had had a "real" job before. In fact, I think I was the first one they hired into management who wasn't a friend or relative. I went to work for them at the ripe old age of 28 – at that time I was a young, up-and-coming upstart. It was later on at Celestial that I became the conservative old fart.

Be a Consistent Partner

When I was with Celestial, we initially got all our herbs from Eastern Europe, the Sudan, and essentially the markets closest to Germany, where the industry was really based. We were very instrumental in directing those crops worldwide – getting hibiscus in China, rose hips from Chile. Peppermint now is actually coming out of Oregon from a former Celestial employee, who grows the best peppermint in the world there. That was a matter of getting farmers to consider alternative crops that would be value driven, where you *know* your supply relationship. You were there in good times and bad times and not just when it was a good crop. You were a consistent buyer, offering people American dollars.

It was quite exciting to work in the Third World, because you felt you were doing something good.

I remember when we first started opening trade with China. These people's itinerary must have been Washington, D.C., San Francisco, and Boulder, Colorado. It was very strange, but they came to Boulder because we gave them hard currency for an agricultural commodity – and that was very instrumental. I don't know if we were as successful in replacing opium poppies in Thailand, but we did work with many different countries around the world to get these crops closer to Colorado, where we were blending our tea. It was quite exciting to work in the Third World, because you felt you were doing something good in giving people hard currency to improve their lives. That was very gratifying.

When I joined Celestial and then Horizon, they were both doing about $3.5 million. Now they're both well in the $100-plus million. When I was with Horizon Organic Dairy, Horizon was really a virtual company – we did have some cows, but for the most part we were a brand that bought milk from farmers and then got other manufacturers to process it organically and make organic milk, butter, cheese, and organic nonfat milk powder. It was quite a challenge because the conventional world has dairy production defined pretty well in terms of value, but there were no values established in the organic world at that time. It was difficult getting manufacturers to understand what organic was all about and how they could comply. I think it was a different challenge getting conventional dairy farmers to consider organic as a way to utilize their capacity better; that's changed over the years. Where initially we might deal with suppliers who weren't that high quality or sophisticated, now they are able to introduce products like organic baby formula because there are enough organic ingredients and people to do that.

> When I was with Horizon Organic Dairy, Horizon was really a virtual company.

Focus on Partnerships

Horizon is both a virtual company and a marketing brand, utilizing the manufacturing capabilities and distribution relationships of all kinds of people, from agricultural farmers and suppliers to very sophisticated UHT (ultra high temperature) pasteurized manufacturing facilities. Building a company like this started out as an idea, and now it's a $250 million brand with essentially no manufacturing at all. It was all developed through partnerships with suppliers.

One of the things I learned at an early age was what I call the first rule of engineering: "Never make anything you can buy." Your suppliers can tell you an awful lot about the things they do, because they're specialists and know how to modify formulas to make things taste better. There's quality to everything, and you've got to figure out where your positioning is for your brand and how you want to do that. At Horizon, we introduced organic orange juice, and we knew it was going to be expensive. Therefore, we had to make sure we delivered quality. A supplier will tell you it's going to cost more, and maybe most of his or her customers aren't interested in that, but Horizon was a unique customer that was very interested in how to make a higher-quality product.

> Building a company like this started out as an idea, and now it's a $250 million brand with essentially no manufacturing at all.

Don't Reinvent the Wheel

I think a lot of people beat themselves up and try to reinvent the wheel when suppliers have already learned where the pitfalls are, how to make the product better, what the costs are, and what you need to do. That relationship is invaluable in terms

of product development and even merchandising and marketing. When you want to do promotional packs – whether single-serve sizes or sample sizes to put the product in front of your consumers – these vendor relationships are critical.

In the organic market, we started right with the farmers and the land and how the land is handled. Then we went on to explain to many of these manufacturers that the rules are not that onerous if they make a commitment to doing it. They solve these problems, and those who are willing to do it benefit from the growth of an entire industry. I'd hate to have to compete with the Procter & Gambles and the Kraft Foods of the world on price. You can't win that game, so you'd better find another point of differentiation for your product, whether it's organic or quality or however you're going to differentiate it. Many of these smaller suppliers can help you with that competitive advantage.

You'd better find a better point of differentiation for your product.

The Power of Consolidation

I look at what's happened in America primarily because of retailers like Whole Foods. It's really changed the entire relationship of natural foods. For a company like Horizon Organic Dairy, it was impossible to have a national brand of milk; it was all regional brands.

With Whole Foods and other companies like it being national, Horizon could build a national brand and eventually solve the logistics of supply cost-effectively. That consolidation hasn't occurred yet in Europe. But as the world changes, one door closes and another door opens. Seeing how the industry's evolving and how those suppliers are emerging, maturing, and consolidating is going to dictate who the winners are going to be down the road.

> Everybody's working with people who know more than they do about certain things.

Everybody Is in Sales

I guess we're all always selling something – whether it's community, nonprofit charitable giving, or networking with the right people and expediting problems. Everybody's working with people who know more than they do about certain things, and whether it's outside consultants or vendors, these are great sources for improving and developing new relations further.

I remember that before Kraft bought Celestial, I was always getting questions like, "What's going to happen when Lipton gets into the herb tea business?" and I'd have to think about it and write some of the risk factors down. After having been involved with a company like Kraft Foods, I should have realized that Celestial had nothing to worry about. In fact, it turned out to be the best thing that ever happened to Celestial to legitimize the category.

At a company like Unilever or Lipton, right before you get fired you get assigned to herb tea – you know that if you were any good you'd be running one of their other businesses, but the herb tea category is still viewed as the weed that grows by the

swamp. This business was not important to them; therefore, the best people weren't assigned to it. If you're at Kraft and you're part of the "Miracle Whip Savings and Loan," your decision has to be, "Is the coupon 25 cents or is it 50 cents? And God help me if I screw up this business, because it's been around for 50 years." That mentality doesn't really create innovation and creativity. In fact, it breeds it out. You have more people at the highest levels of the company and they all say the "right" things. The employees see that risk taking is usually not rewarded, but failure to take risks and not getting into trouble often are rewarded. That's what they see, and that's what they do.

> The smaller entrepreneurs win the game by innovating and looking at smaller niches.

Look at Smaller Niches

Typically, large companies try to use their clout to drive a better deal on price, as opposed to the smaller guy who's looking for their insight, direction, help, and support to create a point of differentiation and an opportunity that other people haven't seen. If price is the primary issue, that's unfortunate. The large companies copy well, and then they use their clout to drive the price down. The smaller entrepreneurs win the game by innovating and looking at smaller niches.

I've been in the industry now for almost 30 years, and it just continues to get better and better. I mean, the stuff we used to have to put up with! Now if you want organic milk or organic yogurt, or you want a 1 percent fat level, in quarts – it's there. Amazing. It's everywhere. But that's great, because that's how we're changing the world, the way America eats, and the way it grows food.

Tools

❶ Focus under the Radar – The opportunity to innovate is all around us. Get out and go deep into the market for new ideas. Barney has made a great career in the natural foods business. Before Whole Foods and Wild Oats were national chains, no one took the business seriously. Now, everyone wants to be involved. By getting under the radar and out in front of an opportunity, you can co-create innovation with your suppliers and customers and stay ahead of the curve.

❷ Don't Reinvent the Wheel – Every time I think I have a new idea, I find someone else who has been thinking similarly. Instead of trying to reinvent the wheel, get out with your suppliers and figure out where they see opportunities. What do they think could be done differently in the marketplace? This dialogue can be a source of much inspiration for co-creating innovation.

❸ Find Unique Relationships with Suppliers – Barney has pushed the envelope with many of his suppliers over the years. Instead of asking them to produce a product at a certain price, he has had to convince suppliers, like farmers, of the benefits of changing their philosophy on how things are made, as in the case of organic farming practices. Think about your suppliers. Instead of a transaction-based relationship, can you develop a truly co-creative relationship?

❹ Focus on Differentiation – We all work in an environment where the time from product innovation to commodification is becoming ever shorter. By having deep relationships with your suppliers, you can focus on unique ways of differentiating your product innovation to slow the crush of decreasing prices. Barney focused on quality and organic at Horizon. What can you focus on with your suppliers to differentiate your innovations?

❺ Look to Small Niches for Opportunities – Many great ideas for innovation start out in a small niche that nobody sees or understands. Just look at the Internet. Part of your innovation process should explore relationships with new (or existing) suppliers that are working on interesting innovation themselves. Create the kinds of relationships with them that encourages you to get the first look at their thinking behind innovative processes.

❻ Get Out and On the Ground – For Barney it was traveling the world, teaching people how to grow the kind of herbal tea ingredients he would buy. Go out and learn how your suppliers' suppliers are making their products. Can you bring new ideas to these upstream suppliers that will give you an advantage in your innovation process?

❼ Always Sell – I had a wonderful art professor in college who was a famous public space artist, designing large sculptures and installations for parks and corporate headquarters. He said one of the reasons he decided to become an artist was that he hated the idea of sales. He said it took him a decade to realize that he had chosen a career that was actually all about sales, selling people on the merits of art and competing with other artists for an installation. He told me that, in retrospect, he would have spent less time selling if he had gone into business. Selling is a fact of life. We all have to sell people our ideas, whether it's our customers, our boss, or our families. Co-creating innovation takes a lot of selling.

Interaction

_____

_____

_____

_____

_____

_____

_____

_____

_____

_____

_____

_____

_____

_____

Develop New Relationships

How does your company view your suppliers? Are they your partners? Do you meet with them regularly and have open discussions about how well your buying process meshes with their production process? Can you bring a product problem to them for a solution, a big challenge that would dramatically help you co-create innovation? What steps can you take to get their creative juices flowing?

Resources

1. Organic Vintners Web site: http://www.organicvintners.com.

2. "Food Porn" by Seth Lubove, *Forbes*, February 7, 2005, 50. Lubove focuses on organic foods offered by Whole Foods Market retail stores in the U.S.

3. "The Green Machine" by Daniel McGinn, *Newsweek*, March 21, 2005, E8. Another interesting story about Whole Foods and the natural foods business.

4. The Organic Trade Association Web site: http://www.ota.com/index.html.

5. The Organic Center for Education and Promotion: http://www.organic-center.org.

6. "Networking and Innovation: A Systematic Review of the Evidence" by Luke Pittaway, Maxine Robertson, Kamal Munir, David Denyer, and Andy Neely, *International Journal of Management Reviews* 5/6, no. ¾ (September 2004): 137. A good look at business networking and the importance of innovation.

7. All About Tea Web site: http://www.teausa.com/. If you've ever had any questions about tea, you'll probably find the answers here.

8. Farm Aid Web site: http://www.farmaid.org. This is a great organization that supports family farming.

9. *Marketing, Morality and the Natural Environment* by Andrew Crane (Routledge). An overview perspective of green marketing.

10. *Strategy and Enterprise Value in the Relationship Economy* by Bruce W. Morgan (Van Nostrand Reinhold). Morgan explores understanding the power and value of "relationship capital" and maximizing its potential.

11. *Making Niche Marketing Work: How to Grow Bigger by Acting Smaller* by R. E. Linneman and J. L. Stanton (McGraw-Hill). This is a classic book on niche marketing.

12. *The Causal Structure of Long-Term Supply Relationships: An Empirical Test of a Generalized Transaction Cost Theory* by Gjalt De Jong and Bart Nooteboom (Kluwer Academic Publishers). An academic look at creating more powerful supply relationships.

13. *The Dynamics of Industrial Collaboration: A Diversity of Theories and Empirical Approaches* edited by Anne Plunket, Colette Voisin, and Bertrand Bellon (E. Elgar). The authors explore interfirm collaboration.

When you meet Pat Keane, a cofounder of PM Gear, the first thing you realize is how passionate he is about what he does. Heck, he calls himself a "Maggot"; that seems pretty passionate to me! Another thing I really like about the company's perspective is its real focus on acting as the conduit to help push the culture forward — in this case, the backcountry ski culture. This energy and perspective is not unique; every industry, from software to automobiles, has small companies owned by passionate customers who have made their passions a business reality. But the guys at PM Gear have followed a creative path to take them where they are today.

While this happened a few years ago, our networked society has put PM Gear and its ski-customers-turned-business-owners into direct competition with bigger, more established brands. Some people inside larger organizations might think that their customers couldn't possibly start competing with them. However, you only have to look at Microsoft and the threat that open-source software has provided it to realize that none of us is immune. In this day and age, with our deepest secrets being shared online and access to our suppliers and technologies no longer unique, the only way to survive is to engage customers and their cultures in the process of co-creating innovation. Whether you are PM Gear or IBM, you have no choice if you want to keep up today. This means being open, sharing both your successes and your failures, engaging in your culture in a very real, participatory way, and often operating at the speed of light.

This is the second business enterprise I've been involved with that's grown out of a message board community. The first involved testing a new ski I found in Switzerland and holding an online contest at *Powder* magazine's Web site, Powdermag.com, for the top sheet graphics of the ski. The response and quality of submissions were overwhelming. I then sold some of the skis to the community. The experience demonstrated amazing potential for the development of a business with, and within, the online community. There were already successful ski and ski accessory online stores, but none seemed to have its finger on the pulse of this worldwide brotherhood of skiers that was evolving. We tapped into a general vibe where everyone was a good skier, cool, and trend setting. Since they all hung out online at Powdermag.com, they became known as the Powder Maggots. That's where our name comes from – PM is for Powder Maggot.

It was also obvious that the brain trust encapsulated within those electrons had the potential to engage in a business enterprise and deliver the products this diverse community wanted, something that the rest of the skiing world would notice. We wanted to make PM Gear available at affordable costs and grow the business out of that because, frankly, on the Internet and in the ski world everybody knows who the Powder Maggots are. They're a rather infamous and a pretty active community of several thousand die-hard, hard-core skiers. There's a lot of power there – good people with a lot of good ideas and money. I put out some feelers on the message board to see if a handful of others thought an online "Maggot" enterprise would fly. We were all investing either cash or sweat equity. The first time the owners of PM Gear all actually met each other was at our first company meeting, and that was about six months into concep-tualizing everything.

There's a lot of power there – good people with a lot of good ideas and money.

We started out as an online retail store with only a few very high-quality items for extremely good prices. Not long after that, still in the early days of the company, a guy who had developed a new kind of ski sent me a pair and I checked them out. At the time, it just didn't seem like anything we wanted to do, but last summer he called me and asked, "Do you know anyone who can make my skis this year, because the guys last year blew it?" As opportunity would have it, I had just met a group manufacturing snowboards here in Reno, Nevada, and I said, "You know, I think that would be me." So I went and talked to the guys who were building the snowboards and asked, "Can you guys build skis?" and their response was, "Oh yeah, sure, no problem."

This guy needs 100 pairs of skis, and as I'm bro-kering the deal I see the potential to design a ski for PM Gear and do another 100 there. So we contracted out to build 100 for this guy I had never met. Then, since we weren't going to make enough money on his deal alone to finance building 100 skis, we went online and started talking to people on the message board, saying, "Hey, what do you want in a ski? What length would you want, what width would you want, what do you want a ski to do?"

Those initial designs were completely based on feedback from the message board. We ran surveys, we polled everybody, because to make multiple lengths or multiple dimensions of the ski can triple the cost. The question was, How do we hit the largest part of the market that we're aiming at? So we just asked them. We had a poll and based on the information we got back, we chose the length of our ski. The same for the dimensions and the construction characteristics and the flex of the ski – we just discussed it with these people. This is a really diverse background of people – doctors, PhDs, lawyers, ski bums (literally, some of the best professional skiers in the world are on there on a regular basis), and just the whole gamut of American society who just happen to share the love of skiing.

Community Spirit
So once we finalized the design, we took a prototype to Mt. Hood on the Fourth of July (the Maggots have an annual get-together there every year) and invited everybody to come and try them. We had probably 35 pairs available – everybody skied the prototypes and gave their suggestions online. A lot of people offered feedback to Sean's questionnaire – he did it because his specialty is psychology – and that gave us a lot of information on what people thought the ski was, what it should be, what it could be, and so

> Initial designs were completely based on feedback from the message board.

on. We made modifications from that, went forward, tested again, and then let people know we were going to go ahead and manufacture this ski and offer it at $450 – if people ordered now to help finance the whole gig. Based on our promise that we were going to give people a great ski, just those words and the whole community spirit behind it, that is what made it all possible. We turned to our customers to finance our business.

Unfortunately, we hit a major snag in the manufacturing process. We partnered with these guys building snowboards and gave them the dimensions for the ski, but they didn't know how to shape a ski core, which is the most integral part. So basically they gave us a snowboard core in a ski. Even though the dimensions and the side cut and everything else about the ski were great, we discovered that this snowboard core design would break down with extended use. We had a product failure at the end of August or early September that we had to overcome before going into production in October.

> It was a real stroke of genius for us, because it was just pure honesty.

Pure Honesty

The whole thing is covered in three articles – if you go to *Powder* magazine's home page, there are three articles specifically about the prototype testing at Mt. Hood and in Argentina. The last article chronicles our current manufacturing woes. It was a real stroke of genius for us, because it was just pure honesty. It's written in a very forthright way that, when we first did it, really made us cringe because it was so honest. But the feedback from people was really phenomenal. We offered to refund people's money if they were upset about the delay, but they said, "You know what, this is really cool – the whole idea, the way you've been honest about it, the whole nature of your company – and we're going to stick it out for as long as it takes." When you read those articles, especially the one called "The Ski is Born," you get more blatant goddamn honesty than you've ever seen from any company in your life. But for us, it's a hell of a lot easier to tell the truth than lie.

Right now, we're basically at the factory every day cracking the whip to get skis out to the people who have paid. That's our number one priority in life right now, getting the product to the people who are expecting it and making sure that it is the best possible product. That's all; that's just job one. It's even hard to look at the future, because our obligation now is so intense. Without that kind of credibility, we are nothing.

We basically put a bunch of designs up online and people voted on them, and we went with the one that got the most votes.

Let the People Vote

There are other ways we've used our connections with customers. One is the top sheet design of the ski. Since we've always been more performance oriented and focused on the way the ski works, the graphics have been kind of an afterthought but obviously still important. So we created some designs and also asked one of the guys from the board who happens to be a graphic designer to come up with a design. Then we put a bunch of designs online and asked people to vote on them, and we went with the one that got the most votes. That was another way we capitalized on the resources and information available from the people in this community.

Word of Mouth

This connection to our customers is who we are. It's what we are – our fingertips are on the pulse of the future of skiing. We're using this "new" marketing strategy called "word of mouth" – the idea that a business can grow based on just spreading the word – and we spread the word lots of different ways. Everybody who is a part of this community and owns our skis is out there working for us, because they're excited about what we're doing; they're into it, and they talk to people about it.

We're pretty involved in guerilla marketing, too – when a pair of skis goes out, so do about 30 to 50 little business cards. Then when people who buy our skis are riding the chairlift and somebody asks about the skis, which is inevitable, they hand them one of the cards. It's got our logo on it, as well as the graphics of the ski, and it basically says: "Thank you for your interest in these skis. You're receiving this card because a bro thought you would be worthy to ski the Bro model. This ski is available only on the Internet and through word of mouth – the price is right, and the choice is yours." It's signed "the Bro Model Team" with our Web site address. We feel the business card really captures the spirit of people who like to believe they're part of some clique or community. It's very noncorporate in a time when people are so tired of corporations and the ugly things they do that it is kind of refreshing.

They're excited about what we're doing, they're into it, and they talk to people about it.

Opportunities Are Everywhere

For us, there is also a spiritual aspect to innovation. We believe innovative thought is created through opportunities and also through the awareness of those opportunities. For our company, it's about how we happened to meet some guys who built snowboards and just happened to get a call from a guy looking for 100 pairs of skis, and it clicked right then and there. Even though we didn't have the money to do it, we saw how to put it together. The opportunity was there, and it was a matter of just chasing the son-of-a-bitch to make it happen, to instantly formulate a plan, to see the possibilities, to do an almost instantaneous feasibility study of it all, and to talk about it with all the partners at PM Gear.

> We are the future. We move at light speed. We have to.

The Networked Company

We have our own forum on the Internet because everybody in this company is living in different places – Utah, Reno, Seattle, Sacramento, Lake Tahoe, Salt Lake, Oregon. We've got one guy who's a soldier in Iraq. So we have our own chat board just for the company to discuss things like this. It's our primary means of communication. We do use some e-mail, but mostly we just use a message board where we can bring up a topic related to anything from marketing to money to design to manufacturing, and we just discuss the hell out of everything there.

Move at Light Speed

Our company is a really bizarre cross section of humanity that probably wouldn't have gotten together without the Internet. None of us is a businessperson by training. It was just a unique combination of events and people that wouldn't have occurred otherwise. Without the Internet, we'd be standing on the street corner hacking skis to ten people, and that's just not viable. Five to ten years ago, anybody who wanted a pair of skis had to go to a store and buy them. Now they're coming to our store online. We are the future. We move at light speed. We have to, and that's one of the things that is really unique about us – it's only by moving at light speed that you see certain opportunities.

❶ Participate in the Culture – We all get so busy working that we forget why we're doing the work in the first place. Think about setting some time aside each day to participate with your customers and their culture. This might be going to a conference, reading weblogs, or just hanging out in a coffee shop. People want to participate with you in a dialogue if you give them the opportunity.

❷ Let Customers Build the Product – At the heart of co-creation is the question, "What do you want?" So much innovation is produced in the spirit of what we think customers want. Giving customers the ability to create their own innovations doesn't work in every industry, but the spirit of co-creation and participation goes a long way in earning every customer's trust. At the very least, you'll get a lot of great feedback and some fresh ideas.

❸ Let Your Customers Finance Your Innovation – When you are involved with the community of your customers and they feel that they have become psychologically invested in your innovation, offer them the opportunity to help finance the project. Get them stoked, then get them to participate financially; if you can engage your customers' passion for the product, their preorders can act as your production money.

❹ Be Honest about Your Failures – It would be challenging for anyone to write about their own innovation failures in a public setting such as a magazine. It would be tough enough to do this postmortem, but it would be extra difficult to do so right in the middle of the project. However, by rising to this challenge honestly and openly, your company will appear to be more human, inviting a more human response from your customers and the culture.

❺ Leverage Word of Mouth – How many companies print business cards specifically meant to allow customers to spread the word about their excitement for the company's product? Think about ways you can make it easier for happy customers to communicate and share their positive feelings.

❻ Create More Opportunities for Innovation – By making connections, learning, and being in the culture of both your products and your customers, opportunities will present themselves. Keep your eyes wide open for those opportunities. Deeply explore them. You never know what might be created.

❼ Move at Light Speed – Today's networked world moves at light speed. As all of us have seen, when customers have either a good or bad experience with a product, they can communicate it very quickly, radically changing our opportunities and reputation. The only way to survive is to jump into the river and start traveling at the speed of light yourself – you must be willing and able to act on a moment's notice to maximize the opportunities and possibilities that come your way.

Interaction

_____
_____
_____
_____
_____
_____
_____
_____
_____
_____
_____
_____
_____
_____
_____

_____

_____

_____

_____

_____

_____

_____

_____

_____

_____

_____

_____

_____

_____

_____

_____

Let the Culture Create Itself

Are you ready to let your customers and their culture define your products? Think about a product you currently have that might not be hitting the mark. Can you ask your customers how to improve it, and encourage them to participate in detailed conversations to actually do so?

Resources

1. PM Gear's Web site: http://www.pmgearusa.com

2. "Maggots Assault Mt. Hood on July 4th to Test New Maggot Ski" by Pat Keane, *Powder:* http://powdermag.com/features/news/maggotassault072204.

3. "The Refugio" by Pat Keane, *Powder:* http://www.powdermag.com/features/onlineexclusive/refugio091304/index.html.

4. "A Ski Is Born" by Pat Keane, *Powder:* http://powdermag.com/features/columns/keane_120804/.

5. *Unleashing the Ideavirus* by Seth Godin (Do You Zoom, Inc.). Seth wrote the classic book on the Internet's ability to propagate ideas.

6. "The Hidden (In Plain Sight) Persuaders" by Rob Walker, *New York Times Magazine*, December 5, 2004. This is an interesting article about BzzAgent, a company that recruits consumers to spread word of mouth about products completely on a volunteer basis.

7. *Beyond the Brand: Why Engaging the Right Customers Is Essential to Winning in Business* by John Winsor (Dearborn Trade Publishing).

8. "Web-Based Marketing: The Coming Revolution in Marketing Thought and Strategy" by Arun Sharma and Jagdish Sheth, *Journal of Business Research* 57, no. 7 (July

2004): 696. The authors discuss the emergence of reverse marketing, customer-centric marketing, and adaptation in the context of marketing theory and practice.

9. "Evolving to a New Dominant Logic for Marketing" by Stephen L. Vargo and Robert F. Lusch, *Journal of Marketing* 68, no. 1 (January 2004): 1. Vargo and Lusch talk about new perspectives that have emerged and have a revised logic focused on intangible resources, the co-creation of value, and relationships.

10. Guerilla marketing: http://www.gmarketing.com. This is a Web site set up by Jay Conrad Levinson, who first coined the term "guerilla marketing." The site offers many articles, links to books, and other interesting and useful information.

11. "Controlled Infection! Spreading the Brand Message Through Viral Marketing" by Angela Dobele, David Toleman, and Michael Beverland. *Business Horizons* 48, no. 2 (March/April 2005): 143. The authors discuss the use of viral marketing through electronic communications to trigger brand messages throughout a widespread network of customers.

12. "This Is One Virus You Want to Spread" by Erin Kelly, *Fortune*, November 27, 2000, 297. Kelly writes a good primer on viral marketing on the Internet.

I met Jake McKee when he commented on my blog http://www.beyondthebrand.typepad.com. I was running a contest, The Audible Response, and Jake entered. When I went to his blog http://www.communityguy.com, I liked what I saw there. Here was a guy who was truly passionate about community. What a great person to be involved with Spark.

During the day, Jake works at LEGO Group as its global community relations specialist, focusing on the adult market. As Jake says, he's not a manager of the community: "The company's community interaction isn't about management, because it can't be managed – it can't be controlled; it can be encouraged and can maybe be guided or possibly influenced here and there." In playing the role of guide for LEGO, he has set a very clear mission for himself with his motto, "Everybody goes home happy."

With this focus on facilitating the relationship between LEGO and its adult customer community, Jake has set up an early warning system that any other company would love to have. Most people think about community in the context of word-of-mouth marketing, but as Jake reminded me, "You can't build word of mouth, you can only set up the right environment for it." His ideas about being a guide, hiring passionate outsiders, focusing on personal relationships, and experiencing the good, the bad, and the ugly are important ideas when thinking about the ideas of community around any company and its products.

Irecently changed my title to be more appropriate. I had the word *manager* in my title, which just didn't make any sense in a community. The company's community interaction isn't about management, because I can't manage it or control it. I can encourage it and maybe guide it or add some influence, but I certainly can't manage community. I don't think anyone can. So I am the *global community relations specialist.* My responsibility specifically is to act as a bridge between the company and its adult enthusiasts. Some of these people have grown up on LEGO; some have come to it as adults. All of them use LEGO bricks as a creative medium, so instead of doing woodworking or painting, they're building sculptures and models and whatever suits their creative impulse. Obviously they're a good group of people to pay attention to, because their average spending per person per year is so much higher than the kids' would be. But, relatively speaking, the numbers are much, much smaller than the overall buying audience of LEGO products.

Connect with Key Voices

In the early days, we got a lot of questions like "If adults are only about 5 percent of your market, why are you paying attention to them?" We had a couple of answers to that question. Number one, obviously they do spend 5 percent of the money, which can be the difference between a great year and a bad year. But also, while it may be only a small percentage of adults spending a certain amount, the number of people they tell about their experience is pretty significant, not to mention the brand ambassadorship they carry to the rest of the world through their public events or just by putting images on their cubicle walls.

> While it may be only a small percentage of adults spending a certain amount, the number of people they tell about their experience is pretty significant.

They also convey a really interesting message in a way that we could not. When we say you can build anything with LEGO bricks, the whole consumer base really says, "Sure you're gonna say that; you're LEGO – that's what you do." But imagine 10,000 people going to a LEGO train show, walking through a local mall, and seeing a 30-foot by 30-foot train layout. Every time, they stop and say: "Wow, this is great. How long have you worked for LEGO?" And these adult consumers say they don't, that they just go to the store and buy LEGOs like anyone else – that's the kind of thing that gets the consumers interested. It's a pretty powerful message in and of itself.

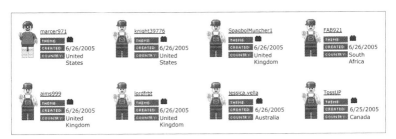

Establish an Early Warning System

We've also learned that these people are our early warning system. There was a lot of questioning up front about whether we should really listen to their feedback because they're really not our target audience – even though they were good, and it was good that they were a market for us. People wondered how much overlap there would be because they had their own issues and interest levels and things that they really liked or didn't like that were significantly different from kids' likes and dislikes. And there are certainly times when we look at what they say they like but what the kids say they hate, and that's the stuff we filter out. But 60 percent or more of the time the adults are saying the same thing as the kids; they're just saying it six months in advance.

Lately, as we've gotten other colleagues interested in working with the adult fans and really believing that the "early warning system" is true, we've had a number of different projects where we've gone to a small group of the adult fans and said, "We're interested in having you participate in the product development cycle." Right now, there are three active and ongoing projects with a small group of adult fans as part of the development team for that particular product. It's pretty amazing.

An example from last year is the LEGO Factory product. It started out as a concept of doing a product line based on the idea of microscale buildings. We worked on this internally with our design team, and our designers are brilliant world-class artists, but we weren't sure if it was going to actually work. So a guy from our concepts department, which is set up to look at product development in the one- to three-year time

> Sixty percent or more of the time the adults are saying the same thing as the kids.

frame, came to me and said, "We need some input from outside the company but we need it quickly – in three weeks." We knew that this kind of time frame would never work with the kids, so when he asked if the adult fans would be interested, I said, "Absolutely."

Guide the Community

I knew a guy in the community who built this type of microscale model all the time. I said, "Hey, I've got this project going on; I can't really tell you much about it except it will be really cool. I'd love to have you lead it." And he said, "That's great. Let's do it." So he found ten of the right people to participate and contacted them on behalf of LEGO. Then we decided on the final group together, and he was responsible for moderating the group. These guys were spread all over the U.S. and Europe. Some of them had posted online before but had probably never met. They conducted the whole group online without ever physically sitting down together.

They conducted the whole group online without ever physically sitting down together.

In three weeks, that group generated more content than any of us imagined was possible just by our saying, "Here's the concept. What can you build in microscale?" We didn't show them any examples of what we'd done; we didn't give them any details other than a very short half-page description of the concept. They generated a huge amount of models, which they gave to the guy in the concepts lab. He was able to make his presentation with all their content and say, "This is a concept worth pursuing, and this one isn't. If you're worried about whether or not normal consumers are going to believe in this – boom, here's your answer."

Having this kind of consumer-driven group gave us the benefit of a hands-off approach. What I didn't want to do was jump in myself the moment I entered the room, with everybody turning to me and saying, "Well, what do we do?" So having a consumer group work through the problems was part of the answer set as much as the result itself. It was interesting for me to watch just what they were discussing and the ideas they were driving and all agreeing to.

> It's not about bashing people over the head; it's about getting them to experience in some way the idea of building with LEGO.

A Dating Relationship

When I talk about the relationship I have with the fan groups and they have with me, it's like a dating relationship. If I show up on a date and I'm absolutely perfect, my date doesn't think, *Wow, this is so great – he's perfect!* She thinks, *What's wrong with this guy?* Her defenses immediately go up, and she assumes I'm hiding something. When companies do that same

#4888 Ocean Odyssey

thing, you immediately think they're just spinning it, that it's just marketing crap and you don't need to pay attention to it. But when you actually start to have an interaction with them, then you have a relationship. Sometimes it's bad, sometimes it's good, but at the end of the day, as long as it's more positive than negative, that's what it's all about. That's what people really believe; that you're not just messing with them or trying to get them to buy something. LEGO.com is not really just an overt sales channel. Of course, at the end of the day all of our content goes to supporting sales because that's what we're here to do. But it's not about bashing people over the head; it's about getting them to experience in some way the idea of building with LEGO. Or it's about playing a game where you're using bricks to do a certain thing. But it's definitely more than just a glossy brochure in the form of a game.

Really focus on why your customer interactions are working or not working.

I talk about this "dating relationship," even though it may seem kind of strange at first, because it works so damn well. If you're trying to form a relationship of some sort, whether it's a product purchase or a consumer-to-company long-term interaction, you're hoping to form a bond between two parties. Again, everybody has to go home happy. If the fans I'm working with are constantly coming away with the feeling that they're being used, then I'm not going to be able to tap into them very much longer. By the same token, if they're not delivering much to me, then I'm not really going to be that interested in working with them. There's a give and take, just as in any relationship.

If you said to me that your company had decided to form a bond with your customer, to break down the wall between the outside and inside, and you asked how to go about doing that, I'd say to really focus on why your customer interactions are working or not working. For instance, why would you have call centers outsourced to India? For most companies, customer service is the only point of consumer contact, and it's being outsourced. It makes about as much sense as having someone you don't know hang out with your wife while you're out bowling. And as you leave, you say, "Oh, by the way, while I'm bowling, can you really work on my relationship for me?" You wouldn't do that in your personal life. Why would you do it in your business life?

> You need personal relationships — both on your teams and with your customers — to inform what you're doing.

Bring Passion to What You Do

It's also really important to find employees who love what they're doing, whatever that particular thing is. In my case, I didn't necessarily need to come from the LEGO community and be an adult fan first, but it certainly helped. You need to get somebody who really understands. You can't just take one of your standard marketing people and throw them in the mix and say, "All right, have fun." That seems fairly obvious, but you always hear people talking about just transferring another brand manager over to fill a position. I probably wouldn't go that way. I'd get somebody from outside the company, or I'd get somebody in the company who's not part of marketing or PR, someone who just loves what they're doing and can't wait to get a shot at the big time, so to speak.

Interaction versus Marketing

Once you have the right person, how do you actually make it work? So many people get in this ad agency mindset of trying to start up a campaign or do something on a short-term basis. It really bothers me because it doesn't work for this sort of thing. You need personal relationships – both on your teams and with your customers – to inform what you're doing. The difference between community interaction or marketing (or whatever you want to call it) and traditional "sit up in your office and throw out a campaign" type of marketing is that personal relationship. There's also the belief of way too many marketers that consumers are incredibly stupid. Marketers have absolutely zero respect for consumers. There's an assumption that unless they just bash people over the head with a campaign, there's no way consumers are smart enough to figure it out on their own. It's not that consumers aren't smart enough; it's that they're just not interested.

People often talk about "building" word of mouth. You can't *build* it; you can only set up the right environment for it. What is happening with the companies that will do well in the next five to ten years is that these companies are reducing the barriers between people inside the company and consumers outside the company. A lot depends on what your definition of *community* is. Really, it comes down to a social connection – it's so much more than just throwing open a message board or a blog and saying, "Okay, it's there. Now what?"

> These companies are reducing the barriers between people inside the company and consumers outside the company.

Tools

❶ Let Everybody Go Home Happy – I love Jake's motto! It's all about getting everyone involved in the community, from customers to suppliers, while ensuring that everyone is excited to be involved and their needs are being met.

❷ Be a Guide – Jake's distinction of letting go of the management paradigm is an important one. As we all learned in navigating the waters of dating in high school, you can participate in and perhaps guide a relationship, but you certainly can't control it. Instead of managing the relationship with customers, think about being their voice inside the walls of your company. Allow for members of the community, both inside and outside the company, to take self-guided explorations.

❸ Form a Community – While lots of companies think about and even say they have formed a community around their products, many times this "community" resides in boxes of warranty cards that have been unopened for years. Think about ways you could form a community of customers and suppliers. Focus on personal relationships. Think about how you could support your community by sharing information and building space, both online and off, to facilitate gathering.

❹ Form an Advance Warning System – Once you have steps in place to form a community around your company, think about it in terms of a strategic advance warning system. How can you use the community, whether it's 10 people or 10,000 people, to give you a strategic competitive advantage?

❺ Define the Relationship between Company and Community – For many companies, like LEGO, it is impossible to start the journey of building a community in the confines of the current company structure. Try taking a small group of people and allowing that small team to engage and start to build a community with customers without the usual corporate pressures. Only after the community gains some momentum should you reintegrate it into the company itself and make it a part of the organization. Remember that community is about establishing long-term relationships, not just creating a new marketing campaign.

❻ Keep Your Customers Engaged – The one thing I've learned from writing a blog is that it's relatively easy to get people excited and engaged initially, but it's another thing to keep them engaged over the long haul. Once you start the process of community building you have to be committed to creating new reasons to stay engaged. Run contests, connect customers to other customers, and create fresh content.

❼ Experience the Good, Bad, and Ugly – I like Jake's analogy that engaging in a community is a lot like dating. At first, people are giddy to be involved. After a while, the humanness of relationships begins to emerge, including insecurities and disappointment. That's all part of the game. To gain the most from a community, you've got to be committed in good times and in bad.

Interaction

_____

_____

_____

_____

_____

_____

_____

_____

_____

_____

_____

_____

_____

_____

Build a Community

Build a community. Start small. Find ten passionate customers who want to be involved with your brand. Who are they? How can you help bring them together to form their own community?

Resources

1. The LEGO Factory: http://www.legofactory.com. This is LEGO's cool community Web site.

2. "Brand Community" by Albert M. Muniz Jr. and Thomas C. O'Guinn, *Journal of Consumer Research* 27, no. 4 (March 2001): 412. This is one of the first academic articles to introduce the idea of brand community.

3. "Building Brand Community" by James H. McAlexander, John W. Schouten, and Harold F. Koenig, *Journal of Marketing* 66, no. 1 (January 2002): 38. The authors discuss the idea of a brand community from a customer-experiential perspective, in the fabric of relationships in which the customer is situated.

4. "Living the Brand" by Anders Gronstedtm, *Communication World* 21, no. 5 (September/October 2004): 14. This article presents information on how to turn frontline employees into brand ambassadors.

5. "Teens As Brand Ambassadors" by Valerie Seckler, *WWD: Women's Wear Daily*, November 18, 2004, 12. This article presents the findings of the study "Brand Marketing to Teens: Why They're Worth It."

6. "Relationship Marketing and Brand Involvement of Professionals Through Web-enhanced Brand Communities: The Case of Coloplast" by Paul Houman Andersen, *Industrial Marketing Management* 34, no. 1 (January): 39. The author talks about the advantages of Web-enhanced brand communities as a lever for relationship-marketing communication.

7. "Keeping a Sense of Community Alive" by Kim Hanson, *Strategic Communication Management* 8, no. 4 (June/July 2004): 6. The author talks about the importance of the sense of belonging to a shared community in an organization.

8. "Can Customers Replace Marketing Departments?" by Alan Mitchell, *Marketing Week (UK)* 27, no. 30 (July 22, 2004): 34. Mitchell comments on the issues related to the strategy of companies making customers brand advocates in Great Britain.

9. "All Hail the Consumer Matrix" by Stephen Seth, *Brand Strategy*, October 2004, 44. Seth discusses consumer relations strategies.

10. *Emotional Branding: The New Paradigm for Connecting Brands to People* by Marc Gobé (Allworth Press). Gobé discusses the power of emotions when it comes to branding.

11. *Customers Are People: The Human Touch* by John McKean (John Wiley & Sons). McKean writes about the history of business as it has come to adopt a more customer-centered approach toward marketing and product development.

12. *The Play Zone: Unlock Your Creative Genius and Connect with Consumers* by Lewis Pinault (Harper Business). Pinault looks at the importance of play at work.

13. *Fan Cultures* by Matt Hills (Routledge). This book is a comprehensive overview of fans and fan theory.

The whole world of blogging and its implications on the co-creative process have intrigued me for quite some time. When I published *Beyond the Brand*, I started a blog to accompany the book. My subsequent, active participation in the blogosphere has changed my ideas about how to interactively engage in a relevant dialogue with people.

When I was working on a couple of technology questions for my own blog, I came across Stonyfield Farm's blog site. Since 2004, Stonyfield has been publishing five blogs, including Baby Babble, a daily weblog "Where parents can meet up, rant, offer and seek advice, or just tell us their trials and triumphs"; Strong Women Daily News, "The latest news and insights from our Strong Women partners"; The Bovine Bugle, "Daily moos from the Howmars Organic Dairy Farm"; The Daily Scoop, "Daily life at the yogurt works, and daily ways we try to nurture and sustain the environment"; and last, Creating Healthy Kids, "Daily updates from our Menu for Change healthy food in schools program."

Christine Halvorson, Stonyfield's chief blogging officer, tells us in her interview that Stonyfield's CEO, Gary Hirshberg, initially drove the idea of using blogs to connect with their customers and the culture (no pun intended) surrounding organic yogurt. In a recent *BusinessWeek* interview, Hirshberg said: "If you're going to go into this as a marketing device, be careful. That's just not what it is, and if you treat it that way consumers will see through it. You have to be willing to let go and allow a really honest expression of genuine things that are going on."

Blogging is still in its infancy, but when it comes to creating a culture around your company that can give you a platform for dialogue and innovation, it holds a great deal of potential.

Christine Halvorson — Develop New Connections

We launched five blogs on April 1 of last year, so we just celebrated our one-year anniversary. It's been great fun; I have to say that before March of last year, I had barely even heard of blogs and definitely had not blogged myself. They were the idea of our company's CEO (affectionately called the "CE-Yo"), who was quite enamored with the technology. He had heard a lot about it – he always has his ears and eyes open for new things, and he immediately grasped the concept that this was a tool that could help his company.

Stay in Touch

Gary had been a little worried because we are an incredibly fast-growing company, and he always liked to say, "We started out with seven cows and a good yogurt recipe." And now we are producing something like 20 million cups of yogurt a month. So he was concerned that we were going to lose touch with our market – if you're a Stonyfield yogurt eater, you're a very committed Stonyfield yogurt eater – and we started out with the organic, all-natural crowd when nobody else did. These people are loyal and committed, and we didn't want to lose them as we grew. So that was the main concern, and what prompted us to latch onto the idea of the relationship-building aspect of blogging.

Get Behind the Scenes

It has been really fun, and I think we have succeeded in connecting our customers to us at another level, in another fun way. One of the blogs that people really seem to have warm feelings toward is the Bovine Bugle Blog – everybody says they just love it. It's direct from the farmer, who hardly ever seems to actually mention Stonyfield, even though he's a provider of our milk. He just writes about his daily life on the farm. So even though yogurt eaters intellectually understand that yogurt is made from milk, and milk comes from cows, and therefore farmers must be involved, they probably don't get to the point of wondering, "Well, what's life like for those farmers?" So he just writes in very excruciating detail, sometimes about fixing a fence or a pump or other times about cracking the ice on the water when it freezes over; people just seem to love it. They have such great comments about it and such warm feelings toward the blog, which we assume translates into similar feelings toward our company.

> These people are loyal and committed, and we didn't want to lose them as we grew.

Have an Opinion

As I've said in other media interviews, I'm not sure this would work if you were producing paper clips for a living, if you did it just to make money and didn't have any particular point of view in the world. But we have the point of view that organics are sustainable agriculturally and environmentally sound; it makes sense that we put ourselves out there and have an opinion.

Make It Real

When I first started here, if I was given any mandate at all, it was, "Please be fun and real and authentic" – those were the actual words the CEO used. He really has built our company on guerilla tactics – that's the only way I can describe it. It was only recently that we even did paid advertising at all. He was always out there sampling at bike-a-thons or accosting commuters in the subways of New York and handing them smoothies; that's the way he has operated. So this was absolutely in keeping with his personality; he does instill in his employees and companywide that fun is part of the game.

I think the fact that we have the blogs at all is an innovation for us, though I can't say it has necessarily created any specific innovations for us. But

> "Please be fun and real and authentic" – those were the actual words the CEO used.

Jonathan Gates / Howmars Farm / Franklin, Vermont

we have been working with that farmer since he's been in business, so when we started the blogs, it became immediately obvious to the CEO that having the farmer write one of them made a lot of sense. So we started with that, and we were four months into it before I realized we didn't have any photos, so we bought him a camera. That really brought it to a whole new level. Once people in the company saw that, they started to say, "Hey, that's a cool idea." They really love getting a glimpse of the farm photographically. That also happens on the other blogs I write. People will now come to me and say, "Hey, this is happening down the hall; shouldn't we take a picture and put it up on the blog?" So internally, all of our employees are thinking about communication in a different way.

Both Inside and Out

When the blogs were launched, every employee obviously had the opportunity and was given instructions on how to subscribe. I would say that about half of our employees don't have access to computers because they're the ones filling yogurt cups. But many of those with computers are subscribers as well. When we get comments on the blogs – and we

> All of our employees are thinking about communication in a different way.

haven't had many negative comments – employees notice and will talk to me about it, or it might spur a discussion in a staff meeting. Our CEO has been very good about that from the outset; we have a consumer relations line – 1-800-PRO-COWS – and every employee who wants to can get a record of the actual complaint calls that we get. We have a report of all the calls we receive, so anyone can read through it; we do try to share that with the employees.

Build Content

I should back up and talk about the Baby Babble Blog; when we created that, it was an interesting harmonic convergence. We'd long ago had the idea of having a photo contest for babies so their committed parents could send in photographs of their kids. Through the contest, some would be chosen to appear on our YoBaby packaging. The idea was in our company before we had the blogs, but at the point that the contest was launched, we were so inundated with entries, it was kind of a good news/bad news thing. We knew we were going to have great entries in the contest, but we were also going to possibly tick off the other 12,000 parents whose babies were not chosen.

> This kind of thing is so much fun to do, and the technology of a blog makes it so easy.

So we really created the blog first off to not only speak to the very committed segment of our audience but also to talk about the contest and build some interest that way. Then when it happened and we had such a great response, we were able to communicate with all those parents who didn't win and say, "But your baby's photo will appear on the Baby Babble Blog someday." The "photo of the day" in the upper left-hand corner changes every day, and those are all our runners-up. That not only gave those par-

ents a good feeling, but it's also building content for the blog and keeps the excitement of the contest going. This kind of thing is so much fun to do, and the technology of a blog makes it so easy. That's what really appeals to me about it.

Be Active Daily

I was trained as a journalist and did that for four years, and then I worked for several years in government as a writer. After that, I spent seven years as a freelance writer and in public relations, so I think – although I haven't been told this – that I was hired because they could see that I could produce quantity in words. I do sort of approach the blogs every day as if I'm on a daily newspaper: What's the news today? What do I have to do? What would be fun to do? Then I just try to tackle it from there – but speed is definitely a good skill to have.

They saw that we were doing blogs, which at the moment are in the public's consciousness as something that's cool and innovative.

Have a Real Voice

In terms of how the blogs have affected the company and the business overall, it's a little nebulous, like all public relations efforts somewhat hard to measure, but we can quantify how many people have visited the blogs. It's something like 110,000 at this moment,

since we began. In the scheme of things, that's actually not large for us; we have a monthly newsletter that goes out to 400,000. But those 110,000 people saw that we were doing this kind of writing and speaking to people in a real voice. They saw that we were doing blogs, which at the moment are in the public's consciousness as something that's cool and innovative. Even if they're not participating, they'll note that we're doing something that a lot of others aren't. So we can only presume that those people have a warm, fuzzy feeling about us – and that maybe that comes through as they stand looking into the yogurt case at the grocery store: "Oh, Stonyfield – that's the one with the funny blogs!" Our CEO has absolutely said he doesn't care what the return on investment is at this point; we're going to let it run its course.

> We know we have found those committed yogurt eaters and are speaking to them in a new way.

Instant Gratification

Another benefit to the blog format is that it's a great tool for putting up news quickly; despite our size, we're a pretty small Web-based staff. So if there's something that we really think needs to get onto the Web quickly, it's a wonderful way to do that. Even an English/journalism major like me has conquered this technology, and I can do it in an instant while our Web designer is busy working on projects that were due three weeks ago. So that's fun; also, I can see blogs evolving into simply that type of content management tool. Maybe one day they won't be so chatty but will still be an integrated part of our Web site that we use to keep everything dynamic and refreshed. For now, we know we have found those committed yogurt eaters and are speaking to them in a new way. That's just not debatable.

Tools

Develop New Connections

❶ Get Behind the Scenes – Let your customers really see what's happening behind the scenes in your company. Focus on transparency. Even allow them to see what's happening with your suppliers, like Stonyfield Farm does so well with the Bovine Bugle Blog.

❷ Stay in Touch Daily – Part of the magic of blogs is that they are a daily experience. Don't worry about overanalyzing everything you write. Make it fast and timely. It has to have a human fresh voice.

❸ Have an Opinion – If you really want to engage with the culture around your company, you have to have an opinion – the whole idea behind blogging is to voice one. There are many great examples of how bloggers have made a company more human by being willing to express their opinions. Consider Richard Scoble and his blog, http://scoble.weblogs.com. His blogging has single-handedly given Microsoft a more human face.

❹ Make It Real – There is always a faction in any company pushing for more secrecy and control. Let it go! When it comes to interacting with the culture in which you exist and co-creating innovation, honesty and transparency are the only choices. Find someone who is a passionate user of your products, not necessarily someone in marketing or communications departments. And let's face it, when you want authenticity, you can't subcontract your relationship with your customers and their culture to a PR firm.

❺ Both Inside and Out – Remember that co-creating is all about forming an ecotone. When you start blogging, be sure you solicit participation from both company insiders and outsiders. Get the dialogue going.

❻ Build Content – It's easy to hammer out a few words each day; however, content isn't just about words. Think about images and even video. Ask everyone to participate with content. Run contests. Give away prizes. Generating participation in the dialogue will pay off when you are trying to innovate.

❼ Have an Authentic Voice – Authenticity comes from consistency. A blog should exude a personality that gets people stoked to be involved. It's believable and engaging. Having an authentic voice lays a wonderful foundation for co-creation.

Interaction

_____

_____

_____

_____

_____

_____

_____

_____

_____

_____

_____

_____

_____

_____

Develop New Connections

Start a blog. Go to typepad.com or blogger.com and check out how blogs work. After looking at a few blogs, draw a picture of what your blog might look like. Write down the human attributes that your blog should have. Now sign up on either site and get going! It's cheap and easy.

Resources

1. Stonyfield's Web site: http://www.stonyfield.com. In addition to other information, the site also has links to Stonyfield's five ongoing blogs.

2. "Blogs will change your business" by Stephen Baker and Heather Green, *BusinessWeek*, May 2, 2005, 56. This is a great overview of why blogging is important to business

3. *The Weblog Handbook: Practical Advice on Creating and Maintaining Your Blog* by Rebecca Blood (Perseus Books Group). *The Weblog Handbook* is the first book to explain how weblogs work and explore their impact on the media landscape.

4. *Beyond the Brand* blog: http://beyondthebrand.typepad.com. This is my blog and has lots of links to the blogosphere.

5. *Blog: Understanding the Information Reformation That's Changing Your World* by Hugh Hewitt (Nelson Books). Hewitt has been an important voice in the world of blogging. His book is a worthwhile read.

6. "Marketing blogs present new legal issues" by Bart A. Lazar, *Marketing News*, April 15, 2005, 6. The author analyzes legal issues that should be considered when developing a commercial blog to be used as a marketing tool.

7. "Don't Write Off Blogs Yet" by Ephraim Schwartz, *InfoWorld*, April 11, 2005, 10. This is another good source of info about the impact of blogs.

8. "The ethical dilemma of blogging in the media" by Patrick Beeson, *Quill* 93, no. 3 (April 2005): 18. This article discusses the ethical issues of blogging in the media.

9. "The Enterprise Blogosphere" by Michelle Delio, *InfoWorld*, March 28, 2005, 42. This article discusses the advantages and disadvantages of corporate blogs and wikis.

10. "Many Advertisers Find Blogging Frontier Is Still Too Wild" by Jessica Mintz, *Wall Street Journal*, March 25, 2005, B1. Mintz discusses how many companies are wary of putting their brand on weblog Web sites, a new and unpredictable medium.

11. "Year of the Enterprise Wiki" by Jon Udell, *InfoWorld*, January 1, 2005, 38. This article focuses on the concept of the wiki site, which was developed to collaborate with programmers on the explanation of common software patterns.

12. "Three Trends for 2005" by Rich Karlgaard, *Forbes*, January 31, 2005, 39. Karlgaard forecasts two technology trends for 2005: (1) significance of blogs and (2) consumer products being marketed directly to average consumers.

In The End ... A New Beginning

Spark has been a wonderful journey. I hope, on reading this book, you share my sense of feeling energized and inspired in your quest to better understand how to be innovative through co-creation.

At our core, all of us have the innate ability to be innovative. We must free ourselves from the shackles of modern work, focusing instead on recapturing the imagination and creativity that we used as children to frame our worlds. We must strive to be a part of a community that creates an environment in which innovation can become a natural product instead of something forced and painful.

The interviews in Spark demonstrate there are many paths to innovation. There is no formulaic process, just a broad sense of wonder and passion. There are, however, some constants we can see. To be more innovative, think about things in terms of the innovation community. When thinking about you, and your team, create a holistic and balanced approach to innovation. Try to remember to allow everybody, no matter the level of knowledge, to participate in a positive dialogue. Likewise, develop a policy of more open communication, dialogue, connectivity, and equality. Remember to focus on learning and experience versus accomplishments.

When thinking about your company, it's important to remember that innovation is not necessarily

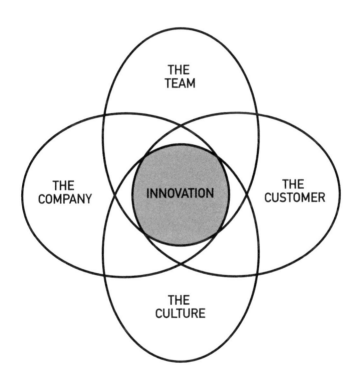

a top-down process, but the necessary support and nurturing must absolutely be top-down. Innovation can spring from any part of the company-customer community, but ONLY if the support and encouragement for this environment exists at every level of the business. Remember to learn from failure, reduce bureaucracy, and encourage companywide communication.

It's also important not to get stuck simply using one method for all your innovation needs. Remember that space does matter a great deal. A company's workspace should be seen as a creative tool, where the cross-pollination of ideas and accidental intersections are possible. Next, fight mediocrity and safety in a way that inspires everyone to be brave. Last, be sure to make innovation iterative and focused on keeping the momentum once co-creation is started.

When it comes to involving your customers, be sure to think about inspiration and not reliance. It's all about progression. And progression is based on immersion. Stop sitting at your desk and spend some time with your customers in the context of their lives. Take a chance and strive to become an inspired protagonist in your market. Have fun by creating a culture inside your company that mirrors your customers' culture. Nourish the playful interaction between you and your customers.

In your interactions with the culture around your company, think about leveraging your relationships with your suppliers in more innovative ways. Develop new ways to engage with your community. Remember, you'll never be able to manage it or control it. Participate in it. Make use of new tools, like blogging, to interact with your culture. Allow the culture to create innovation with you.

The future doesn't just happen in our chaotic world; somebody has to create it. Instead of waiting for innovation to "just happen," I hope this book will inspire you to create an environment, culture, and dialogue that foster a spirit of innovation in all aspects of your business and your life. Good luck creating your own innovative spark.

Thank You

First I need to say thank you to those people who helped me co-create this book. Thanks to Henry Beer, Rob Bon Durant, Scott Bowers, Rob DeFlorio, Adam DeVito, Barney Feinblum, Jeff Garwood, Christine Halvorson, Matt Jacobson, Michael Jager, Pat Keane, Kyle Lefkoff, Jake McKee, Johnnie Moore, Mark Parker, Michael Perman, Marsha Skidmore, and Irene Tengwell, for opening up their lives to be a part of Spark. Thanks to Steve Jenkins, Nadia Kaneva, Lou Patterson, Scott Webber, Annie Weber, and Summer Elton for doing so much of the heavy lifting.

Books like this would not be possible without the inspiration of the Radar team, including Berto Delaroca, Bryan McCarthy, Carol Kauder, Daemon Filson, Dagny Scott Barrios, Dave Kingsbury, Ethan Decker, Josh Harrod, Kim Morris, Kyle McCuistion, Pete Takeda, Stacy Valencia, and Troy Mault.

Last, and most important, thanks to Bridget, Charlie, and Harry for their unwavering love and support.